D1116519

Personal Relationships, the Handicapped and the Community

THE CONTRIBUTORS

James A. Loring
Director, The Spastics Society, London
Secretary General, The International Spastics Society

Derek Lancaster-Gaye
Assistant Director (Services), The Spastics Society, London

Sven Olav Brattgard
Professor, Department of Handicap Research,
Gothenberg University, Sweden

John Frederickson
Ministry of Housing, Copenhagen, Denmark

Arie Klapwig
Medical Director, Johanna Stitchting, Arnhem, Holland

W. P. Bijleveld
Director, Het Dorp Foundation, Arnhem, Holland

Margaret R. Morgan, M.B.E.
Head of Social Work and Employment,
The Spastics Society, London

A. H. Sutton

M.-B. Bergstrom-Walan, PhD
Stockholm, Sweden

Inger Nordquist
Secretary, Swedish Central Committee for Rehabilitation

Sven Brant and Torben V. Hansen
Cerebral Palsy Clinic, Orthopaedic Hospital, Copenhagen

H. d'Olivat
Secretary, The Committee for Sexuality among the Disabled,
Amsterdam, Netherlands

Ton M. C. M. Schellen
Department of Andrology and Sterility, R C Hospital,
Sittard, Netherlands

C. O. Carter
Director, Clinical Genetics Research Unit,
Institute of Child Health, London

Personal Relationships, the Handicapped and the Community

Some European thoughts and solutions

Edited by Derek Lancaster-Gaye

LONDON AND BOSTON
ROUTLEDGE & KEGAN PAUL
in association with the
International Cerebral Palsy Society

First published 1972
by Routledge & Kegan Paul Ltd
Broadway House, 68–74 Carter Lane,
London EC4V 5EL and
9 Park Street,
Boston, Mass. 02108, U.S.A.
Printed in Great Britain by
Unwin Brothers Limited
The Gresham Press, Old Woking, Surrey, England
A member of the Staples Printing Group

ISBN 0 7100 7478 6 (*c*)
7479 4 (*p*)

Contents

Part One

The Severely Handicapped in Care and the Community

Part Two

Sex, Marriage and the Heavily Handicapped Spastic

Part One

The Severely Handicapped in Care and the Community

Introduction: Residential care and the adult spastic

James A. Loring

> All happy families resemble one another, but each
> unhappy family is unhappy in its own way
> Leo Tolstoy—*Anna Karenina*

It is sometimes said that the handicapped person living in residential care is the least desirable of a number of alternatives, and that living with the family and in the community is to be preferred. This proposition should, I think, be carefully examined before it is accepted because it is based upon little or no evidence. We are living in a post-Freudian age in which life in the community and with the family is highly valued, where close personal relationships are thought to be of supreme importance, but in which the actual quality is seldom assessed objectively. Many of us both handicapped and non-handicapped have had familial experiences which range from happiness to extreme misery.

One of the main ambitions of most adolescents and adults is to leave the family and very often the community in which they were born, which they regard as institutions to which they would not want to conform; they seek in fact another milieu in which they can develop in greater harmony. We often assume it should be an objective to keep the handicapped within the community and within the family. It would certainly cost the state less, but it does not follow that living in that sort of setting is considered by the handicapped person to be desirable.

It should not be assumed that living in the community will necessarily provide the optimum life for a handicapped person. Living in a residential home can in some circumstances be far more enriching; but it will be a world that he will not be able to structure. He enters what Erving Goffman calls a staff world: a world that can present itself to the outsider as a rational organization operating to achieve officially avowed and approved ends, but these ends will probably amount to the objectives of the staff rather than of the handicapped person. The staff of institutions have objectives and products on which to work and these objectives and products are people. There is a very real danger that people in institutions may assume the characteristics of inanimate objects and be treated as such by the staff.

It is essential that one should be on the look out for depersonalization. The 'efficient' residential home should always be suspect. Efficiency should help the disabled person rather than merely give satisfaction to the staff. Only too often there is a gulf between humane standards and institutional efficiency. The personal possessions of a human being are an important part of the materials with which he builds a self, but as an inmate of a residential centre the ease with which he can be managed by staff increases with the degree to which he is dispossessed of his own wishes. It is not unusual to find in many subnormality hospitals that cleanliness and tidiness are valued to such a degree that it has been felt impossible to allow patients to retain any of their personal possessions, where personal clothing is non-existent and every distribution of clean laundry is a re-distribution of a community wardrobe, not according to ownership, but according to approximate size. Indeed, the conflict between organizational and human interests can be very real indeed. Organizational interests have a deadly logic behind them. For example, Herman Melville in *White Jacket* states that one of the arguments advanced by officers in the British Navy in favour of corporal punishment is that 'it can be inflicted in a moment, it consumes no valuable time and when the prisoner's shirt is put on again that is the last of it'.

Happily we have now moved a long way from problems of this sort, when this approach is compared to the near ideal conditions that exist at Het Dorp in Holland, Drummonds in England, Fokus of Sweden and the Kollektivhusets of Denmark. But the advances that they represent are relatively recent and there are still many bad institutions and a great many indifferent ones. These exist even in some of the most advanced countries, and many do not provide for people of very low intelligence, whereas nearly 25 per cent of all cerebral palsied persons are in that category. It is estimated that one cerebral palsied person in every four has an I.Q. of less than 50 and many of these also have a severe physical handicap. A very large proportion of these are living in large institutions sometimes containing several thousand inhabitants where the conditions are a disgrace to the civilization that claims to provide for them.

Surprisingly there is a significant lack of literature and published research on the subject of residential care for the disabled, whereas there is a plentitude of literature about special education. This is an area in which a substantial amount of research has taken place. There is also some published material about school leavers and their problems, and there has been research in this field. Similarly there is also much published work about institutionalization, but very little about the important work of caring for the adult handicapped outside his own home. It is also worth noting the lack of philosophy in this field and in particular a lack of objectives. In the field of special education there is much discussion about the objectives and about what the underlying philosophy of educating handicapped children should be. For example, some people believe that education should be for its own sake, others that education should have a strong vocational bias, or that the school curriculum should be laced with special programmes to help attune the children to the outside world so that they can better adapt themselves when they leave school. But if one were to ask even the most enlightened who are responsible for adult care, what objectives are pursued in their centres, the answers would almost certainly be vague. For example, many adult centres have workshops attached to them and it is implied that doing a day's work in the work centre is in itself a social necessity. But upon what is this assumption based? Not all disabled people get pleasure from working with their hands and the endless monotony of producing objects in which they have no interest for communities about whom they care nothing can be soul destroying. The profitability of these centres is sometimes marginal and the majority are run at a loss, yet centre residents who are unwilling to go to the work centre are regarded as an 'awkward squad' and possibly in need of psychiatric treatment. It is not so much that taking part in work projects is looked upon as an objective, but rather that the physical structure of the centre has provided a workshop and the belief in the Protestant ethic, 'The devil finds work for idle hands', operates. In fact, there is nothing particularly moral about making baskets or putting nuts on bolts. A great deal of this sort of activity stems from an authoritarian and puritanical structuring of leisure patterns. A handicapped person might be happier reading, pursuing a hobby, listening to the radio or learning a new skill which would make his restricted life more pleasurable. Unfortunately, schools for handicapped children too often regard ultimate employment as the only acceptable objective.

All too often in the field of residential care we find a lack of opportunity to facilitate personal relationships. Whilst many centres are enlightened in this matter the vast majority of institutions for disabled people are so constructed as to make a close personal relationship with another resident extremely difficult. Whereas unhandicapped people seldom find it difficult to make love in private, for handicapped people in a residential centre it may be very difficult indeed, and privacy of any sort is almost impossible, with the result that personal relationships remain undeveloped or if developed have a slightly coarse and comic quality about them. The claim of a medical superintendent of a large institution well illustrates this point. One morning he was approached by one of the residents who was in great distress. When questioned she told him that she had been in the institution for thirty years and she had had a steady relationship with a male resident. For most of that time they had slept together at night in a disused boiler room, but the man had died suddenly and now she was beside herself with grief. On investigation it was discovered that although the staff had known that a friendship existed between the two, none would admit to knowing that this long-standing intimacy had existed. It was an institution for subnormal people which had been grossly understaffed for decades and the staff had no time to interest themselves in emotional problems unless these exploded in violence. It is not only important that all new residential centres should contain adequate facilities for privacy but even more vital that the old ones should be adapted to produce it.

Large institutions provide three major disadvantages. First, they offer a system of block treatment—that is to say a regime whereby all the residents have to do the same thing at the same time. Second, they insist on a rigidity of regime—that is to say a regime which is imposed from above and operated by a hierarchy and can only be varied or altered to suit human needs with great difficulty. And third, they generate depersonalization—the treatment and care of human beings without regard to their personalities and often without regard to their human dignity.

One must not assume that such conditions are necessarily insuperable; it is possible to reorganize large institutions in such a way that these three characteristics do not operate to any important extent. This has been demonstrated by research in the United Kingdom by Tizard, King, Raynes and Yule, in their account written in 1900 'Investigated Management of Children who are inmates of Residential Institutions'.

What then should be the objectives of residential care? In the case of those with a moderate handicap they may be quite plain, particularly when rehabilitation is possible, but where no substantial rehabilitation is possible and where the prospect is life-long containment in an institution what should the objectives be? Should they be to occupy the handicapped person? Should they be simply to care for and maintain him? A popular reaction could well be that the best objectives should be to enable the handicapped person to lead as enriched a life as possible, but what is a rich life? Ideas will differ and in a residential centre with 100 people ideas will be even more varied. The issue here revolves round the problem of objectives and stems to a great extent from our regarding ourselves as being responsible for solving the problems of the handicapped, forgetting that we ourselves are part of the problem. Before one can begin to decide upon objectives, one must surely consult the handicapped to find out what they consider those objectives should be. A severely disabled person was recently discovered in a subnormality hospital who had been admitted at the age of seventeen as a spastic imbecile. It was many years before it was discovered that he was of very good intelligence by an imaginative charge nurse who then taught him to read and write. His physical handicap remains gross but he has been able to write a short book which has been published and he has developed an impressive knowledge of music. In his case the institution started off with the objective of containment but by something of a miracle the objective had to be changed to enable him to undertake journalism and musical criticism. The point here is that the dynamic of the institution was hostile to the man and he was saved from a slow emotional and physical death more by luck than design. It would seem, therefore, that if one were moving towards a definition of objectives one would rate very highly the need to extend fully both physically and mentally disabled residents, and not one in which the needs of the staff and the history of the institution dictated the dynamic.

One must consider too the matters of architecture and design. Residential homes for the disabled should not be designed primarily on the basis of supposed physical needs.

The width of doors and the gradient of ramps are very important but they have only a marginal influence on people's lives and a preoccupation with them can cloak the real issues that determine success or failure. Human relations are critical matters and it is the quality of these relationships that count and determine whether the centre is a good one or not. Superficially the residents in a centre for the disabled may appear to have many of the same characteristics but in practice they are very different people and staff should encourage that differentiation. Civilized society strives to enable all its members to attain their full potential and this should be an aim for the disabled. They should not be expected to play a submissive and passive role although it is very easy in an authoritarian structure to force them to do so.

Four primary needs that are common to everyone are:

(1) The need to be accepted in family or community as a human being.
(2) The need for security and position.
(3) The need to enjoy the confidence and respect of those about us.
(4) The need to exercise ability and self-expression on an individual basis and not to live as a stereotype.

Bricks and mortar can help to satisfy these needs but only an enlightened and compassionate staff can ensure their fulfilment. Too often we are expected to express surprise and approval of architectural wonders by persons in charge of new buildings but as we are taken around it becomes painfully obvious that at the personal and emotional level the scintillating design has already become a mausoleum of human aspiration. The human spirit is held as if a fly in aspic. We must never become bedazzled by gadgets and electronic devices. If only a small proportion of what is spent on these and bricks and mortar were devoted to staff training and the evolution of a career structure such as that which exists in education and medicine there would be a great accretion of happiness to the disabled.

The problem is one about human beings. It is only about the problems of the disabled in the sense that we, ourselves, are part of that problem. It is about the potential that exists in each one of us, able or disabled, about the ways in which we can use this potential. Those of us who work for the disabled are very fortunate indeed because the opportunities for giving and caring, for developing our potential for loving others less fortunate than ourselves, are so much greater than if we were in ordinary occupation, but the authority we have over other human beings is great and its power very frightening. We must examine how we are to use it and to re-examine our own roles and objectives and our motivation.

I

The United Kingdom approach to residential care

DEREK LANCASTER-GAYE

Residential care, like country pubs, double-decker buses and the right to chain oneself to someone else's railings is a typically British institution, and it is the approach to this emotive and vital subject in Great Britain that we now consider. I intend to illustrate the impact upon these disabled people who, for one reason or another, are unable to lead a life of relative independence, independent by care at their own hands or those of a parent or relative, of inadequate state provision in this field and the role that these inadequacies have imposed upon the Spastics Society in the United Kingdom.

It is probably a cold fact of life in most modern countries today that the cost of the social services, both those that are provided and those that have yet to be introduced, greatly exceeds the funds that are available. In the past the battle of competing financial priorities at both national and local levels has been fought with little evident emphasis on the growing need for improved residential care facilities—improved that is in terms both of quantity and of quality. Britain's National Health Service with its annual cost well in excess of £1,000m has been on a financial tightrope for several years and the present rate of inflation has done little to ease an already acute situation. The need to increase efficiency within the service has, quite properly, placed greater financial burdens on the local authorities who are now required to cater for people such as the aged and more of the chronically sick, and the Chronically Sick and Disabled Persons Act has quite properly added to these burdens. So great has been the urgency of these improvements to the hospital system that it has been necessary for the government to impose certain priorities in local authority development. And it is as a result of these priorities that many of the services for the disabled have had to remain at standards of twenty years ago.

It is also characteristic of the British way of life that local authorities have a degree of independence and autonomy that many might envy. But it is this very independence of action that has led to the fragmentary and varied service available in different parts of the country. With a local authority system of finance that relies very largely on local rate demands, it is not surprising that those authorities have sought to meet the demands for long-term residential care in a manner that has had more regard to the costs involved than the very special needs of certain sections of the disabled community, including spastic persons. Where 'homes' have been provided from this source it has seldom been in a manner that has coped with the intellectual, physical and community needs of the handicapped. By the same token, lack of finance has tended in the past to mean second-rate buildings, a lack of staff with the right training and stimulus and long waiting-lists.

Of course, sooner or later public conscience and the very size of a problem tend to influence state provision and it is fair to say that in spite of the acute shortage of ready cash, many more local authorities have concentrated on this problem in the past few years. More places have been made available and plans exist for many more centres in the future, but it is evident that the problem of sheer weight of numbers will remain with us for some time to come. There is also the quality of care to be considered. Too often in the past the care of the severely physically handicapped has been custodial in approach, care meted out in circumstances all too reminiscent of the subnormality hospital. The centres, often catering for upwards of seventy residents, have been introspective in orientation, isolated from the community that they serve and devoid of the special needs of the cerebral palsied resident. A general lack of understanding of these special needs, of the physical provision, the role of the therapies and the often complex emotions of those who do not have the ability to communicate either with the staff or with their fellow residents have led to standards of care that are below the quite reasonable expectations of the potential residents for whom the alternative of placement in hospital or a home for old people holds even less attraction.

And so it was against this background of too few places, too little money and too little understanding of the needs of the spastic person that the Spastics Society entered the field of residential care. Just how valid were some of the early decisions made by the Society may be questionable. Whilst many local authorities had a demand too small to justify any sort of special provision, the Society was able to establish residential units on a national basis and to provide accommodation for persons from many parts of the British Isles. The principle of establishing services for whom the only beneficiaries were spastic was at that time secondary to the urgent need to provide more places. There was an emotional need to be settled and the Society embarked on the development of a series of residential centres expressly for this purpose. It did so with typical 'charity' beginnings. The emphasis was on 'bulk' provision. How many places could it secure for how small an outlay consistent with certain standards of care? The requirement was to scatter centres around the country to ensure as far as possible that residents would at least be within striking distance of their homes and relatives. And, of course, there was the need to provide a variety of facilities to cater for the special demands of intellect, degree of handicap and age.

To take into account these three factors alone presented the Society with quite a problem—a problem of size for in fact the Society was seeking to provide acceptable facilities for the total spectrum of handicap and if realistic communities, realistic to the residents and to the staff who were to care for them that is, the number of places and the number of centres were to be quite substantial. Purely from the intellectual point of view, this meant that the Society was concerned separately with those who were regarded as educationally subnormal, those of average intelligence more or less and those who might be classed as 'bookish' and keen to live in a more educationally stimulating environment in which further studies might be pursued.

At this stage both cost and speed were relevant and it was not unnatural that in making this provision the Society turned to another British institution, the large country mansion, several of which were converted and enlarged to provide residential care for communities of some forty to fifty residents. The advantages were obvious. The premises offered an abundance of space and plenty of room on the site for expansion and the development of the industrial activities that have played so important a part of the centres and the daily lives of their residents. The disadvantages were equally obvious. They were usually sited in the country remote from the local community where staff were difficult to find. And there was always a built-in presumption that the residents approved of the country life.

But at least the decision enabled the Society to produce many places quite quickly and with them the specialized facilities so badly needed. They succeeded in establishing what came to be regarded as a viable and compatible community that offered to the resident companionship in a secure home not too far from his own home: companionship with those in a more or less similar intellectual group, and in an environment where the occupational activities were able to provide a continuing stimulus and sense of purpose. The work centre sought to cater for the various physical and emotional abilities of the residents, with a variety of original products that often had some relevance to the local community and an equal variety of work that had been subcontracted from light industrial firms in the area.

And through the work centre it was often possible to introduce a small group of non-resident spastic people who would attend on a day basis. Generally the Society's centres were allowed a more generous staffing ratio, especially in the care field, where a very high proportion of the residents were committed to the wheelchair and were unable to attend unaided to the normal daily conventions of toilet, bath and feeding. And it was possible too to introduce a degree of specialized medical and psychiatric supervision where this was necessary backed by social work and psychological support. Physio-therapy and speech therapy were also made available on a level that was realistic to the age of the residents.

The question of age was a difficult one. In the early days, admission to these centres was sought for a wide range of age groups and this posed the question of whether there was a case for what might be called 'all age' centres or whether the Society should seek to establish centres with a particular age characteristic. 'Young' centres and 'old' centres, for instance, where the design of the building and the nature of the activities might be more closely related to the needs and to the wishes of the residents. In the event, the Society provided some of each, though in retrospect the case for anything but an 'all age' centre, with the possible exception of a centre for elderly spastic people where the case rests on the obvious design advantages, is probably a weak one. Generally, the Society accepts responsibility for the permanent care of its residents—the home it is providing is home for all time in normal circumstances—until, that is, the resident is in need of continuous nursing care, usually as the result of advanced old age, senility or physical deterioration at which point in time one would expect the resident to be transferred to a more suitable placement. But old age in itself and without the attendant problems of senility is not the basis of a transfer elsewhere. Death in any close community is never a pleasant circumstance, but it is a perfectly natural one and it is surely fitting that it should happen in home surroundings. Experience has shown us, however, that in some cases the elderly resident expresses a preference for transfer to an institution more closely geared to their needs, to the quiet and tranquillity that can be an essential part of old age.

The Spastics Society has been able to undertake much pioneer work in the United Kingdom since its inception some twenty years ago. Whether the units have been residential centres, schools, training centres, workshops or hospital units, the units themselves have been the first of their kind and the Society has had no model on which to base planning. Generally, the results have been successful, but it is understandable that mistakes have been made and these have made it possible to improve subsequent planning in the hope that the same mistake has not been made on more than one occasion. Much of the Society's earlier work has been concerned with the conversion of existing properties and the physical limitations of this policy will be understood by anyone who has been concerned with this form of development. Notwithstanding the fact that developments undertaken in this way are quicker to materialize, they are invariably more expensive. Whilst they may have a maturity of age lacking in a new building, they are often far from the 'ideal'.

Most of us will have been anxious at some time or other to achieve something approaching the 'ideal' assuming always that we have been able to identify just what the ideal really is. Unfortunately, as this is so frequently the consensus of the objective views of the planners, the practical views of the staff and the subjective views of potential residents or of those speaking on their behalf, the end result may fall a long way short of this ideal in design terms. For this reason the development of the Society's first purpose-built residential centre at Drummonds in Essex was an interesting experiment. It was interesting not only because of the decision to build an entirely new environment for a group of severely disabled adults, but because that group and the staff were already in existence, living in a centre that had to be abandoned some two years ahead. It was possible therefore for full consultation to take place and for many of the wishes of the residents to be taken into account in the planning. Drummonds is a single-storey building providing accommodation for about fifty residents of both sexes, two-thirds of whom had already lived in the neighbouring centre less than a mile distant. The total development cost in the region of £333,000 (at 1967 prices) and the cost factor inevitably had to be taken into account when considering the design of the building. There has been much contention, especially amongst the architectural profession, about the principles on which the unit was designed as the scheme relied upon the provision of multiple bedrooms for the residents—rooms for two, four or five people with only a small proportion of single rooms. In some measure this decision was based on the fact that many of the residents had already lived together on this basis and had even expressed a preference for this principle in the new building. Account had also been taken of the theory that a multiple bedroom enabled a variety of different disabilities to share a room and so increase their collective independence. In the event, once the advantages of single rooms, with the privacy and relative independence of action and thought that these bring, had been fully appreciated, it was seen that multiple bedrooms were not quite so popular as had been imagined.

But weighed against the many disadvantages of old buildings in which adaptation and ingenuity have had so significant a part to play, the new centre with its purpose-built adjoining work centre were infinitely to be preferred. It is nevertheless an experiment the Society is unlikely to repeat for its present approach to long-term care has now taken a more definitive form. At about the time Drummonds was completed the Society's finances were less able to cope with the growing demand for a wide range of developments in other fields and it was necessary to re-assess priorities.

This re-assessment resulted partly in a slowing down of the Society's residential centre development and it was necessary for the Society to close waiting lists and to look to local authorities to do more to find a solution to this continuing problem. Certainly local authority developments have increased during the past few years and whilst this has eased the demand, it has at the same time had the effect of increasing the degree of handicap of the residents for whom the Society is asked to make provision. The proportion of wheelchair cases, of those requiring near total care and of those presenting some special problem such as speech defect, in the Society's centres has increased.

These changes in the Society's approach to residential care were due in part to the limits of finance, and a change in demand accompanying local authority development in this field. There was also a growing awareness of the need to look more closely at the quality of care that was being provided and the quality of life in the Society's centres from the residents' point of view. It was difficult to find a case for the large communities of fifty people or more, especially where these had been established in a very rural community often remote from the limited activities of an English village. Centres that had been established in a more urban setting tended to be more popular and it was probably fair to assume that their urban siting had something to do with that preference. In any event, staff were generally more difficult to recruit and to keep in rural centres and it was often necessary to provide special transport services to convey staff to and from the centre. Though there will always be a demand for residential staff vacancies in the care field, the demand is very much smaller than it used to be and the ability to accept day staff enables one to employ people from a wider range of backgrounds free of the interactions of a closed community. And there was, of course, the need to study the promotion of greater independence amongst the residents in the attention to the daily necessities of life and at the same time to make the life of care staff easier and more acceptable. With the growing severity of handicap it becomes less easy to provide a community of residents not only balanced on an intellectual basis but balanced in such a way that the staff were able to cope with the increasing demands made upon them.

In short, it was felt that future developments should lay greater emphasis upon the domesticity of the setting in which care was to be provided and upon a greater independence. There has been a strong case to support the present policy of establishing smaller units based in an urban community, near to local shops and community facilities and in such a way that the unit relies almost entirely for its work and entertainment upon that community and not upon the facilities that would have been built-in to a rural development. The result is a unit, relying almost entirely upon non-resident local staff, providing for some twenty-five residents, all with quite severe physical handicap, the majority of whom will go out to attend a local work centre provided by the local authority. Such a centre now is able to relate its provision much more closely to the needs of the individual resident and his bedroom or bed-sitting room is designed to meet the anthropometric needs of the occupant and provides the opportunity for greater privacy and independence.

The Adult House Unit, as it is known, catering as it does for an economic number of residents, and designed on the principles described, is able to provide a more acceptable quality of life for many of our residents and in such a way that many of the centres will be nearer the homes from which they come. It should also be possible to arrange for residents to transfer from one unit to another where this preference is seen to be realistic whilst the larger number of smaller units will make it possible, in theory at least, to match the potential resident more closely to the community and to the staff in any particular unit.

Probably the corner stone of the Society's residential provision for spastic adults has been its development of small hostels. These are usually existing private houses situated within a normal urban community that have been converted to accept between ten and fifteen spastic residents. The handicap of the residents is less, of course, than it would be in a large residential centre and by the same token the staffing is smaller, usually limited to a resident housekeeper and a small domestic staff. Emphasis is on greater independence and an even closer community integration. Of the ten or more residents, a small number would normally be able to go out to some form of open employment, the remainder relying on the provision of a work centre either at the hands of the local authority or the Society. The mix is usually a happy one and one calculated to encourage as near normal an approach to living as is likely in present circumstances. The Society has also been able to experiment with an interesting variation of the hostel, by building one specially in the grounds of one of its larger centres and making the accommodation available to perhaps eight of the residents on the basis that this would offer them a greater degree of independence and accommodation for a married handicapped couple. The hostel is equipped with catering facilities for those who are able to use them, though experience shows that the majority tend to rely upon the main catering facilities offered by the centre for all but special occasions. In all cases if any attempt is to be made to provide a degree of integration for the residents with the local population then an adequate transport system, capable of dealing with the most seriously physically handicapped and their wheel-chairs, must be provided.

Integration with the local community is a desirable goal but it is a matter of degree and the Society has had to admit that for the majority of the residents for whom it has sought to provide long-term care, total integration in the community is both unrealistic and impossible, if integration is seen as an individual situation. The issue really is whether or not it is possible to integrate a small community of disabled persons as a unit into the community. Much will, of course, depend on the size of that local community, its location and the acceptability of the group of handicapped persons. Compatibility is seen as an essential element in the composition of this group both to provide a balanced community and to ensure more acceptable relationships within that community. Much importance is placed on initial assessments undertaken by the Society's professional panel when intellectual and physical capacity are taken into account as well as social orientation. Thus provision is made for the lower intellectual groups, but seldom are places for these groups made in residential units intended to provide stimulus for the more bookish residents. At a time when care staff are difficult to find there is also a strong case in favour of mixing residents with a less severe physical disability with those who are in need of continuous care and whose physical handicaps are considerable.

It is necessary to emphasize where appropriate the thinking that is behind the policies the Society has adopted. We have progressed from what has been described as 'bulk provision' to an approach that is more concerned with improving the quality of life and it is understandable that this will mean changes in approach. Custodial care, with a few exceptions, is now a decade or two behind us, but one must still come to terms with a number of important problems many of which have yet to be identified. How realistic is it, one must wonder, that centres are established to accommodate only one type of handicap? Do the cerebrally palsied really wish to live together any more than fishermen or farmers? Of course there are practical limitations which for the time being dictate that this must be so. But we are dealing with people who have points of view, who have likes and dislikes that they are becoming more ready to voice. We have not yet reached the emergence of a 'residents union' but we certainly have residents' committees and study groups in which the residents are represented which operate with varying degrees of success.

Management of the larger residential centres run by the Society has been in the hands of special committees working with the wardens. Their concern has been the day to day management of the centre. Now, as an experiment, the possibility of an entirely new approach to the same ends is being tried out through the medium of a working group in one centre studying the quality of life within that unit. The group includes a number of senior staff from the centre, a social worker and several members of the old management committee which the group now replaces. The residents will, of course, be involved with this working group and it is hoped that a new approach to the daily life within the centre will emerge in which both minority as well as majority voices of the residents will have a contribution to make and as a result of which better communication will foster closer understanding between residents and staff.

It is, of course, inevitable that within any residential community such as these relationships should develop between residents that lead to close friendships and to engagements. Only more recently have the issues of marriage been considered seriously. Whilst the proportion of residents who come anywhere near to 'potential marriage' is small, it is probable that one of the factors involved is the problem of finding suitable accommodation within the residential community for a married couple. Much has yet to be learned about the practical problems that will follow from the provision of married accommodation within a residential centre and much anxiety has been expressed about the consequences attendant upon the birth of a child to such a married couple. Various approaches to this issue are being adopted within the Society's centres and these include the provision of purpose-built accommodation for married couples adjacent both to residential centres and to hostels where both independence and support can be obtained when it is needed and to the provision of an entirely separate residential unit. It is perhaps significant that the demand for these special facilities shows no sign of growing, which at least avoids the necessity for adjudication between competing applications for limited facilities and the application of a series of subjective criteria to assess which couple most merits consideration.

And now a word about work. It is part of man's evolutionary make up that he works and by working makes some constructive contribution to society. His work has become a discipline upon which his attitude to life depends in some measure. We have tended to assume that the severely handicapped person should want to work as with the ability to contribute something to society will come a sense of dignity and an element of normality. In making available long-term care for the severely handicapped it is fitting that we should consider whether, in fact, our present approach to industrial activity is necessarily the right one and whether there are not acceptable alternatives, acceptable that is in both the social and practical sense.

Residential care is seen as the last resort when family support or total independence are no longer available or possible. The Society has become increasingly concerned about the lack of provision within the housing community to enable disabled people to remain independent for as long as possible. For this reason it established a special housing association recently whose prime object is to promote or establish improved housing for the disabled and their families, but in such a way that they are part of a larger environment that is totally accessible to the handicapped person and in which the total number of dwellings occupied by disabled persons does not exceed a controlled maximum, which is put quite arbitrarily at 25 per cent. Such developments will include practical support in trained hands which can take over when an aged relative has to leave off or where merely nominal support is required to enable someone to retain independence and the dignity that goes with it. Other principles involved are the provision of an element of choice in where to live—a factor that has been so sadly lacking in the past—and the establishment of an environment which is as near normal as possible. For this reason the Society is concerned with any physical disability for which some specific housing or architectural solution is required. The aim however is to achieve an environment not only suitable for the disabled but equally acceptable to both disabled and to the abled bodied. Public recognition of the problems of the disabled in Britain is slow to develop. With the assistance of recent legislation on this subject, however, perhaps public awareness will increase, but it is clear that it will be a slow process and one in which the Spastics Society will have a continuing and a changing role for some time to come.

This is, of course, a situation that will only be achieved by a better understanding of the community at large and by the staff involved in the care of the severely handicapped, many of whom will never be totally integrated in the community. This we shall only achieve by statutory effort and long and patient public education on the one hand and special staff training procedure on the other hand. The Spastics Society recognized this problem early in their development of residential care services and established a staff training college whose courses in residential care are now widely used by different organizations and authorities involved in the field of residential care of the disabled.

But whilst these changes are taking place, one must hope it will be possible for us to learn from the experiences of others and from the disabled themselves just how we are able to continue to improve the opportunity for them to play an acceptable role as members of society, to make decisions and to exercise choice within the limits of their ability.

2

Sweden: Fokus, a way of life for living

Sven Olav Brattgard

Disabled people, like able-bodied, have expectations about home ownership, about finding a satisfying occupation and enjoying the usual leisure activities and perhaps above all enjoying a life of freedom and security despite their circumstances. The Fokus Society supports a philosophy based on these criteria and assists the severely disabled to achieve a reasonable quality of life. Fokus is concerned with the problems of the severely disabled—those who need not only specially adapted flats but also personal help in their daily living activities. The Fokus philosophy recognizes the following basic rights of the disabled:

a. to live under the same conditions and with the same opportunities as the able-bodied;
b. to live in security with access to reliable personal service;
c. to live in a chosen geographical area;
d. to have a choice of suitable occupation;
e. to enjoy stimulating and satisfying leisure activities.

Many people, once they have visited a tenant in a Fokus flat and have seen all the technical design and equipment details, imagine that the Fokus solution is largely an architectural one. This is completely wrong. Fokus is concerned merely to present a way of living. The very well planned flats are only one part of the system. Another part is the service unit. Most important of all is the psychology underlying the idea. This psychology permeates the entire project. The psychological goal is to bring the disabled person into a situation where he has freedom of choice and responsibility for that choice, recognizing that choice is something seldom available to a severely disabled person.

The idea of Fokus in practice

Integrated flats: The Fokus Society has provided fourteen units with a total of 280 flats distributed throughout Sweden. All the units are in major urban areas where cultural and work activities are readily available.

The flats are in houses of flat blocks in residential areas but near the cultural and commercial centres. This location facilitates visiting by disabled and able-bodied alike and by the same token makes it easy for the tenants to take part in activities in the city. In the house the flats for disabled are mixed with flats for non-disabled. From the outset all the Fokus flats are designed with the severely disabled in mind. In this way the disabled tenant is physically and psychologically integrated with normal society, though to what degree depends upon his own wishes.

The Fokus Society rents the flats from the housing company and offers the flats to severely disabled from the entire country. The disabled tenants have to rent their flats on the same terms as other tenants, enjoying the same rights and having the same obligations.

The design of the flats: A special research team elaborated a programme for the design of technically well-equipped and maximally flexible flats. This programme, which is the subject of a special publication, is the basis for the planning of the Fokus flats throughout the country. Experience and the results of research are continuously incorporated in the planning of new flats.

The Fokus flats are planned for single persons as well as for families and have one, two or three habitable rooms.

The distribution of the flats in the first eight cities is shown in Table 2:1.

TABLE 2:1 *Distribution of flats in cities*

City	*Number of flats*	*1 room kitchen*	*2 rooms kitchen*	*3 rooms kitchen*
Falkenberg	14	9	3	2
Kalmar	12	6	6	—
Molndal	14	7	4	3
Umea	32	18	8	6
Uppsala	29	18	8	3
Vasteras	25	5	10	10
Vaxjo	17	14	2	1
Orebro	25	16	6	3
Totals	168	93	47	28

Some of the flats—especially those for the single tenants, involve the use of an all-purpose room. This is made as an attempt to provide a home in which the tenant is always in the centre of the domestic environment, taking part in all that happens around him. Indeed only the toilet is separated from the rest of the flat. All the fittings in the flat are free-standing units. The tenant thus has the opportunity to re-design his own flat according to his desires and the dictates of his handicap. The floor areas of the flats are approximately:

1 room and kitchen	42–50m^2
2 rooms and kitchen	64–75m^2
3 rooms and kitchen	80–95m^2

All the fittings are designed to offer tenants with some kind of physical disability the maximum freedom of movement. Most of the tenants are wheelchair-users and thus in a sitting position, whilst others use crutches and have to work in a standing position. For this reason all fittings in the kitchen and the toilet are flexible in height. An easily operated consol-track system makes it possible to adapt the height of counters, cupboards, stoves, ovens, handbasins and showers to what is best for the tenant.

The plan for the kitchen—like that for the whole flat—is based upon a series of analyses and investigations from the research group at the Department of Handicap Research at the University of Gothenburg. The most suitable kitchen is the angle-kitchen. Ideally the food preparation area is between the water supply (dish-pan) and the stove. In this way the tenant has the most effective working position. Movable pedestals of drawers—preferably on wheels or castors—offer the tenant maximum flexibility of movement and design of layout and with these movable fittings he can always obtain free space under the most appropriate working place—the stove, the dish-pan or the preparing work bench.

Similarly the toilet is planned after a series of individual investigations about the special needs of the tenant. Both the handbasin and the shower are placed on a consol-track system, which allows extensive height adjustment and provides adequate wheelchair access to the basin.

In the flats a wide range of technical fixtures are provided The electrical switches are gathered into units and placed in suitable positions—on the wall, at the bedside, on a movable table and additionally, if required, separate switch units can be connected near the bed or on the wheelchair—sometimes with radio transmitters—so that the tenant is able to open the outer door, control the lighting or call for assistance from anywhere in the flat. All flats have a main entry telephone, an intercom for contact with the service personnel, as well as an ordinary telephone.

The all-activity department in the house: Every house in which Fokus rents flats contains special groups of rooms for different types of activities. These rooms are open to all tenants—disabled and able-bodied. There is a dining room and kitchen for those who prefer to have their main meal prepared for them and served there. There are rooms with facilities for daily physical activities and exercises—rooms equipped with all the essential accessories. There is also a bathing unit—generally with a Turkish bath and a special bath for people with more severe physical disabilities. A special room is provided for those tenants who wish to pursue some kind of hobby. The laundry is designed for use by the disabled and there are rooms for TV, for group play activities, discussions or the casual cup of coffee. All the elevators and main doors are fitted with automatic controls. In fact every kind of technical aid is utilized when it can be seen to provide for the disabled tenant a greater degree of independence in his daily living.

The service system

Important though the design of flats and common rooms is, perhaps more important still is the personal assistance offered for daily living activities by Fokus. The tenant who rents a flat from Fokus can subscribe to a day-and-night service. In this way he will obtain all the assistance he needs and which would almost certainly not be available to him elsewhere.

In these integrated flats it has been found that the most suitable system for the personal assistance for the handicapped tenants is one following these principles. Every tenant who needs more than an occasional helping hand will be given his own individual assistant. This assistant's duty is to take care not only of the tenant, but also to provide general domestic help. Thus, if necessary the assistant will wash his clothes, clean his flat, prepare his food and do the essential shopping. During the time when the assistant is in the flat personal help for the tenant will include such activities as dressing, washing and help with hygiene.

In addition to these individual assistants, service attendants of a more general nature are allocated to each house, whose job it is to provide supplementary help at any time of the day or night. Such staff can be summoned by the special call system whenever help is needed.

The division of this service into two separate groups is

deliberate. First and perhaps the most important is the fact that the tenant likes to have his own individual assistant. In this way he will have somebody who knows his customs, where he keeps his clothes and other possessions, what he likes to eat and will understand all his personal habits. It is thus unnecessary for the tenant to instruct all the attendants in the detailed daily routine. Second is the fact that the individual assistants come in from outside and bring with them a special approach to the problems of personal care for they are neither servants nor nurses so much as friends arriving with news about the world around them. And third is the fact that this type of organization will encourage the tenant to take care of himself. Main service is provided at prearranged times and the tenant must be ready at the appointed hour.

Staff selection for this work is an important matter. Though a nursing background may be useful, the main qualification is the ability and willingness to care for the disabled tenants and this requires an open-minded approach to the problem. To this extent special staff training seems to be essential.

Something to do

It should be understood that the idea underlying Fokus is not limited to residence and service. It is equally important for the disabled to have something constructive to do. All Fokus units are placed in cities where relatively good job opportunities exist on the open market or in sheltered workshops. But work facilities are never provided in the same building as the flats. The tenants are required to travel to work in the same way as their able-bodied colleagues. But it takes time to find suitable employment and some tenants are not successful. The job may not be one they are willing to accept. For them, hobby facilities must be available preferably within the general community but if he likes, opportunities exist for him to pursue his hobbies in the Fokus unit in which he lives.

However, a man cannot live exclusively for his job or for his hobbies. Contact with other people, cultural stimulus and well-planned holidays are also important and such questions play an important role in the planning of a Fokus unit. Everything is done to help the tenant to obtain the stimulus he needs. For this reason Fokus units are situated centrally in cities where a variety of activities is usually available. It is evident that the city must have special transport available, taxis or buses, for the severely disabled. A tenant in one city can, when on holiday, exchange his flat with a tenant from another Fokus unit and everywhere he goes he will enjoy the same service at the same cost.

The tenant

The Fokus Society is principally concerned with those disabled who may need service day-and-night. For those disabled persons who are capable of living in normal and adapted flats with only limited personal help it is possible in Sweden to provide such a service. But this is not the role of Fokus whose units are planned specially for those who have severe physical disabilities. But it must be remembered that a visual assessment of a disabled person is not enough. An inability to move freely is only one aspect of the problem. Psychological problems are another and social orientation difficulties serve only to reinforce the situation. Many disabled persons coming from rehabilitation clinics or nursing homes may well have to start in a Fokus flat and after some months or years they can, if they like, and when they have recovered their self-reliance, take a flat in the open market.

The organization provides flats for both single persons and for families and the system offers the many young disabled a chance of marrying or living together with disabled or able-bodied companions. Families with children are welcome as tenants and the service includes provision for the children.

A disabled person anxious to secure a Fokus flat must apply to a special committee, most of the members of which are disabled themselves. Selection of the tenants is made after analysing the total situation. Unfortunately, the Fokus Society can only cover up to 20 per cent of the need for special flats with service. (It should be mentioned, that in Sweden, the mentally retarded are cared for according to certain statutory provisions in a separate welfare system.)

Some information about the tenants in the 168 Fokus flats may be of interest.

Degree of disability:	
dependent on wheelchair	77%
crutches	14%
need for help with dressing	52%
hygiene	36%
turning in bed at night	18%
Earlier living situation:	
coming from nursing homes	33%
parents' home	37%
own homes or boarding schools	30%

Of those in wheelchairs some tenants are handicapped to the point that they are mobile in their flat only by using Possum operated electric chairs and Possum environmental controls for doors and lights.

Most of the tenants (80 per cent) were pensioners and out of work when they obtained their Fokus flats. In the first forty-six flats—which have been in use now for more than three years—nearly 80 per cent of the tenants are in work or education. This shows that it is possible for many persons with severe disabilities—including those previously regarded as pensioners—to secure some form of employment or occupation and this is essential if any degree of integration in society is to be achieved or normal contacts with others established.

In Fokus units, no restrictions exist other than those common to all tenants in non-Fokus houses. The disabled tenant is an entirely free agent to plan and organize his flat and his routine as he wishes. Within the limits of his ability the tenant in a Fokus flat has to take care of himself and assume complete responsibility for his own life. He is in no way dependent upon Fokus for major decisions. He has, therefore, to rent his flat on the same terms as everyone else and to pay for it from his own funds. However, taking into account the generally reduced economic circumstances of most disabled tenants, Fokus undertakes that no tenant will be required to pay more than approximately 20 per cent of his income, excluding a basic sum of about 6,000 Sw. crowns (£483) per annum. Thus in practice all pensioners, and this means most of the tenants, pay no rent. The Swedish system of low pensions and economic subsidies, attractive though it may seem, creates many problems. The tenants have to take what is given to them and frequently have little or no choice. In most cities where Fokus is established, the local authorities provide rent subsidies for the disabled for their flats. But these subsidies are not enough and Fokus is faced with the need to pay additional subsidies for the disabled. In most places the local authority is prepared to assume responsibility for and to meet the costs of the individual assistants. But Fokus has to assume responsibility for the day-and-night service.

The tenant has to furnish his own flat and if he has insufficient money for this purpose Fokus will help him to obtain the capital required. All tenants have to buy and pay for their own food, and we have seen that help with shopping is provided where required by the service staff. In all of the units it is possible for the tenants to have dinner served in the common dining rooms if they prefer this. The medical care that the tenant needs will be given by the normal community medical service or at hospital. The Fokus Society is in no way responsible for the medical treatment.

A fundamental approach in the Fokus system is one of self-help. This has no reliance on a nursing situation that allows no independence of thought or action. Independence does not flow from a total care situation, but rather from one in which the disabled person is taught and required to take care of himself. But personal responsibility for his domestic and leisure arrangements remains that of the disabled person. Help, such as assistance with contacts in the community, is provided by Fokus when needed, but the onus remains that of the tenant, all as part of the principle of self-help.

Co-operation with the community and organization

The Fokus Society has three management groups. The first consists of representatives of the community; the second is drawn from the organization representing the disabled themselves, whilst the third comes from foundations and societies working with and for the disabled.

The Central Board has the task of directing the work of the Society itself. In each city, where Fokus is established, there is a Local Board and the members of this Board are appointed from the local community, from the tenants and from the Fokus Society. Very close co-operation is thus maintained in all local activities between Fokus and the community. At all stages the tenants or their representatives have an opportunity to make their voice heard and to vote where appropriate.

Before starting up in a city, Fokus has discussions with the local authorities about the location of the unit, and the opportunities for tenants to obtain jobs and education. A very important factor in these discussions is the availability of a special transportation system for the disabled in the city. As mentioned earlier, in all cities where Fokus is established, the community has a special transport system providing the disabled with taxis or special buses for journeys to work, school, cinemas, theatre or visits to friends. The combination of a good day-and-night service at home and a good transport service is vital if tenants are to integrate with the community and to participate in the normal activities that community has to offer.

Frequent daily contact between the disabled and able-bodied residents is essential to an improved understanding of the problems of the handicapped. It is much a matter of mutual education, a process in which children should be involved as well as adults.

The work of the Fokus Society is essentially to be regarded as a complement to the work of the authorities in the community. The real value of the Society's work—apart from offering a new way of life to about 300 severely disabled people—is that it demonstrates to the community, to the politicians and to the general public at large, that even severely disabled people can live a reasonably normal life given such technical and personal support as they may require. Fokus has been able to show that nursing homes or hospitals are not necessarily the right solution. Some day the community itself may be ready to take over the idea and the work of the Society as a part of the total system in a modern society.

Some economic aspects

The Fokus Society was started in 1964. In 1965 it was allocated a day on radio and television for fund raising and that day produced 11 million Sw. crowns (£810,000). With this money Fokus has been able to rent 280 flats in fourteen cities throughout Sweden. Each unit consists of twelve to thirty flats with common rooms, mixed with flats for non-disabled. The number of flats in each unit is determined by the demands made for service. Experience has shown that the best size for a service unit is one supporting twelve to sixteen flats. The Fokus Society does not build any houses or flats, but merely rents the flats from the house-building companies, who obtain from the government a maximum subsidy of 15,000 Sw. crowns (£1,200) for each flat completely adapted for a disabled tenant. If the costs for the flats, garages and common rooms are greater, the company has to adjust the rentals accordingly. The Fokus Society, therefore, has to pay the economic cost of the flats and the common rooms except for the subsidy of 15,000 crowns.

The annual cost for a tenant in a Fokus unit can be

calculated from the figures from two of the cities where such development has taken place, Orebro and Vaxjo. The Fokus unit in Orebro consists of twenty-five flats: sixteen one room and kitchen of 43m^2, six two rooms and kitchen of 63m^2, and three three rooms and kitchen of 91m^2. The area of the common rooms is altogether 316m^2. There are garages on the ground floor. In Vaxjo Fokus rents seventeen flats—fourteen one room and kitchen of 44m^2, two two rooms and kitchen of 60m^2 and one three rooms and kitchen of 86m^2. The common rooms have an area of 149m^2. Parking places with electrical heaters are provided outside the main entrance.

The total rent for the flats and common rooms in Orebro and Vaxjo is 277,000 Sw. crowns (£22,160). This gives a main rent for each tenant of 6,600 Sw. crowns (£528). The tenants pay around 11 per cent. The subsidies from the community and Fokus of some 5,670 crowns (£455) meet the balance. In the forty-two flats in Orebro and Vaxjo live forty-eight disabled people. The total cost for the service staff—the individual assistants as well as the common attendants and administrators—is 557,000 Sw. crowns (£44,560) or 11,600 crowns (£928) per disabled tenant. The total cost for housing and service will in general be around 18,200 Sw. crowns (£1,500) per year. This cost is less than half the cost of that in a modern nursing home or boarding school today. The cost per day is around 50 Sw. crowns (£4) in a Fokus unit. The total subsidies from the community and government are for the rents 122,000 Sw. crowns (£9838) and for the service 109,000 Sw. crowns (£8896). The subsidies from the Fokus Society are around 600,000 Sw. crowns (£48,387).

Fokus—A way of life for living

In the complicated community in which we are living, there are problems for everyone—but far more so for those who are disabled. Three principles seem fundamental. The severely disabled person must have somewhere reasonable to live, something to do and someone to provide personal help. Such a person should be enabled to influence his own life and to make his own decisions. That is what independence is all about. For many disabled the way to that life can be very long and arduous, but it is the duty of the community to make such goals possible. The Fokus Society has shown one way this goal can be achieved for the severely disabled person and his family.

Services for disabled students in Sweden

Whilst most countries make provision for disabled students, the services in Sweden go far beyond the norm and there is some merit in recording here just what these facilities are.

The school system for disabled children and young people. Several possibilities exist in Sweden for disabled children and young people to attend school. As far as possible the physically disabled will use the ordinary school system and be integrated in ordinary classes. They can obtain all the technical aids they need both in the schoolroom and at home, including electric typewriters and tape-recorders. During lessons they can have the support of personal assistants who will help them with writing, with dictionaries and so on. Classes with disabled children are usually limited to a maximum of seven pupils. Where a normal school is not possible, all handicapped—blind, deaf or disabled—pupils have the opportunity to attend special schools or special classes for handicapped children. If they wish and need to do so they can attend school for one or two years longer than children in general.

All these matters are regulated by an Act passed in 1965. The costs and responsibility rest with the community. In this way, each individual has a good chance of obtaining an education to the limit of his capacity. After one or two years at a nursery school, children spend nine to eleven years in the comprehensive school system. This is followed by two to three years in an integrated upper secondary school. This school has three general lines, one preparing for university studies, one more directly for work (vocational school) and one a 'continuation school'.

After the comprehensive school, it is possible to move to a Folk High School (normally one or two years). These schools are all boarding schools. The services offered to disabled university students are available also to disabled students at the Folk High Schools. These services are paid for by the government.

Services for disabled students. Since 1 July 1970 disabled students at every university, school of economics or university-level institute of technology have been entitled to have their own personal assistants. Services can be divided into five categories.

The student unions in Sweden build residences for their members. The unions borrow the money from the state, and every student pays for his own room or flat. In new residences special flats or rooms will be built, adapted for students with different forms of physical handicap. The extra costs of these flats will be paid for entirely by the state—up to 15,000 Sw. crowns (£1,200). Even when an older flat has to be adapted for use by a disabled student, the costs will be paid in the same way.

The state arranges and pays for services to the students requiring personal assistants. The assistant has, for instance, to dress and undress the disabled student, take him to the toilet, buy food, accompany him to the theatre, to shops, to church and so on. These services will be granted to all who need them—those confined to wheelchairs, the blind, etc. Students receive a day-and-night service, and those who need help to turn over in bed get it. The third part of this very complete service is the transport system. Everyone who needs help with transport—the blind, disabled with crutches, those confined to wheelchairs—can travel by taxi or special car for the same charge as an able-bodied student has to pay when he uses a public bus. The transport service takes the disabled from his home to the lecture room and provides for carrying him up and down stairs etc. The fourth service system is assistance with study. This can take the form of personal help to a student who is blind, deaf, or confined to a wheelchair. Someone can help to carry books, read texts, or write figures. As a fifth part of the service for the disabled, there are various technical aids. These are all free, (typewriters, tape-recorders, wheelchairs etc).

How to obtain services. A disabled student wishing to attend a university or institute of technology has to apply for a place at the university, at the desired faculty. If he has sufficient qualifications, all is well; if not, he can obtain permission to take part in the courses. The student then has to go to the student union to apply for a room or flat. He will be given preference in this respect, over other students. The room or flat will be adapted for him, the costs being paid by the state. At the same time, he has to submit a request for personal assistance with the ADL-functions to the State Board for Services to Disabled Students. This board will establish contact with the social welfare administrators in the university city, and ask them to arrange the necessary services. The board has to contact the prefect at the faculty or department and ask for assistance (personal or technical) in his studies. This he will receive from the university, which will also pay for the cost.

Both health control and rehabilitation activities are arranged through the student union health services, or the rehabilitation centres. The rehabilitation service is paid for by the County Council in the student's home district. All technical aids are free, and paid for by the state.

The State Board for services to disabled students. This Board was started on 1 July 1970. It has seven members, all appointed by the government. Its members represent education, social welfare, the County Councils, the employment authorities and the disabled. The Board has to plan the services offered to disabled students, both at the universities and Folk High Schools.

Today, the Board is responsible for about 120 students, half of them at universities. The Board arranges services at all universities (currently in eight places). The disabled student can thus, in principle, attend whichever university he likes. In practice, when the university buildings are not suitable for the disabled, the students choose the university most suitable for them. The Board have no instructions how to act with regard to a disabled student from abroad, though it is likely that this question will be solved in a positive direction.

The financial situation of a disabled student in Sweden. Like all other students, he will receive financial support from the state. This is currently about Skr 8,000 (£640) per annum. He can obtain this sum for four years. Three-quarters of the money he has to pay back when he is earning over twenty to twenty-five years. One-quarter is a grant. If he cannot work and earn money, he is not required to pay back anything.

As a disabled person he can obtain certain additional support, e.g. for one more year. As a student, he can obtain an invalid car from the state. If he has special expenses as a result of his disabilities he will receive financial support from the national insurance system, a maximum of Sw. crowns 3,600 (£288) per annum. Sometimes the student draws a disabled person's pension and will then have his insurance of about Sw. crowns 6,000 (£480) per annum. In this event, his student allowance will be reduced. Those studying for special employment that is suitable for them can also obtain some support from the Labour Market Board.

The disabled student has to pay for his room or flat in the same way as anyone else. He also has to pay for his transport. If he has support for his disability he will have to pay some money for his ADL-services. However, he never has to pay for technical aids or for personal assistance with his studies.

3

The Danish approach to residential care and community integration

JOHN FREDERICKSON

The Housing Committee for the Handicapped

The following pages are intended to provide a picture of the Danish housing philosophy in terms of the physically disabled and in particular to deal with the collective house in Hans Knudsens Plads in Copenhagen which when developed over ten years ago was probably the first building of its kind in the world.

To describe the development in Hans Knudsens Plads as an Adult Centre with the overtones of institutionalization that this description implies is misleading. The collective house is basically intended as a normal domestic environment planned to contain disabled as well as able-bodied tenants but with the superimposition of certain special features to place the disabled on the same terms as the able-bodied.

First it is necessary to consider a few basic statistics. In Denmark there is a population of about five million people. Three-quarters of these are living in cities and urban areas and about one-quarter in rural districts. About 50 per cent of the population live in their own homes. In the years immediately after the war non-profit building societies were responsible for almost half the new house building, the majority of which were flats and apartment houses. The building of single-family houses in Denmark has to a large extent been low single-storey dwellings that are, of course, suitable for disabled persons.

The building of apartments to let has tended to be concentrated in the urban areas, whilst in the rural districts and smaller urban areas there are very few apartments to let, a major problem for the disabled who live in these areas. New building is usually financed through special credit associations, and these are created by co-ordination of the borrowers themselves. The borrowers are jointly and severally responsible for the loans raised. To raise loans it is necessary for the borrower's house to be given in security and the loan is paid in bonds which are sold on the Bourse. Loans can only be obtained up to a maximum of 75 per cent of the building cost including the value of the land. For buildings erected by the non-profit Building Societies the state and the municipality guarantee loans up to 94 per cent of the building cost, the remaining 6 per cent being covered by contribution from the tenants. If some of the prospective tenants are unable to meet the total costs without help, aid can be obtained from the municipality to pay the deposit.

Immediately after the Second World War the financing of new buildings was undertaken by means of government loans for a number of years, but this system has now been abolished.

A number of surveys has been undertaken to illustrate the number of disabled persons and the domestic conditions in which they are required to live. The first survey was made on the initiative of the invalids' organizations in 1955 and 1956, and was taken in a typical urban area and in a rural district. The next survey was made in 1961–2 by the Research Institute set up by the government with subsidies provided by other invalids' organizations. This was a country-wide examination which provided some valuable information about the housing conditions of disabled persons. It is not surprising that a common feature of the surveys was that the handicapped at the time were found to be living under considerably poorer conditions than the population generally, a factor that applied not only to housing generally but also to heating, plumbing, toilet and bathroom design and problems of isolation. Such a situation was only to be expected, for the handicapped belong to an economically deprived group that has little alternative but to accept the cheaper and less suitable accommodation available.

Part of the nation's stock of dwellings will always be cheaper and less suitable and one is bound to question which part of the community is to live in these poorer houses and whether it will always inevitably be those who are hardest up.

Fortunately it has been generally accepted in public debate in Denmark that this group should have special subsidies, and included in this group will be the severely disabled who need a dwelling standard above the average in order to cope with the special problems of disability. On the basis of the different surveys it must be stated that about 3–4 per cent of the population within an area have problems of mobility and therefore need special consideration in terms of building, layout and dwelling design. The Reports from the Institute of Research have shown that about 30 per cent of men and 39 per cent of women over sixty-five years have difficulty in using stairs.

If one adds to the number of persons with such mobility problems people such as children, mothers with small children, pregnant mothers and the aged then one must usually take it for granted that the number of persons who require the same special consideration in layout as do the disabled will be about 10 per cent of the population. The number of persons being severely disabled and wheelchair-bound is estimated to be somewhat below 0.5 per cent of the population.

Organized efforts towards a solution of the housing problems confronting the disabled are comparatively recent and only within the last ten years or so has the necessary legal ground been prepared. After the Second World War, as in most countries, there was in Denmark a considerable increase in the demand for dwellings. Fortunately this was not due to destruction by war, but to the economic crisis of the thirties when too few apartment houses had been erected. Initial housing efforts for the disabled were concentrated on the acquisition of dwellings and the invalids' organizations were especially preoccupied with the economic and technical problems involved. The technical interest was especially concerned with the fact that a dwelling is the basis for the satisfaction of demands for a domestic and family environment, sleeping, eating, security and sexuality. The collective houses with their support services are intended to satisfy or make it possible to satisfy these demands on behalf of the disabled.

The environmental aspect of housing development is at the present time a much discussed issue with reference to quite new urban environments. The demand for freedom of movement, light and fresh air has been considered important, but, nevertheless, the buildings frequently lack the atmosphere and life of an old established development.

Present-day consideration of housing development is concerned mainly with new building and with the fact that good housing design provides the basis for contact between people, and the proper provision of facilities for children. On the other hand the possibility of isolation as well as communication must be considered, especially for the disabled. Further the collective housing layouts and supporting facilities must be undertaken in such a way that better contact will be encouraged.

In many respects domestic developments in Denmark are creating new problems simultaneously with the solution of others. For instance the reduction in the price of a washing machine enables most families to install one in their homes. Naturally this must be seen as progress for everybody, including the disabled, but at the same time this progress also means that the use of collective laundries is diminishing, and with this change comes a diminution of contact and an increase in isolation. The same may be said of the greater availability of the motor-car which has improved transport, but has at the same time increased isolation.

The politics of housing in Denmark can briefly be

summarized as the wish to give the disabled a dwelling where he or she can participate as actively and as fully in the social life of the community as possible, within the limitations which his disability dictates. It has been encouraging that in this way many more disabled people have been made resourceful than we had dared to hope.

Generally the demands that are made with regard to the layout and design of housing are not too difficult to fulfil or too onerous provided they are considered at the beginning of the planning process. For most of the disabled persons with a mobility problem the most important demand has been with regard to the approach to the dwelling and the differences in level, both inside and outside the dwelling, and for the provision of suitable lift access. Other demands have been mainly concerned with the smaller rooms such as the toilet and kitchen, which are so often planned too small, even for the able-bodied. Naturally special attention must be given to the layout of the dwelling if the disabled is wheelchair-bound or has similar mobility problems, but the demands are mainly of such a kind that the dwellings are equally suitable for those without disability and will generally be regarded as an improvement for any occupant of the dwelling.

In Denmark we are of the opinion that integration of the disabled into the social life of the community must be created. This integration can be achieved by making the dwellings and buildings flexible to the greatest technical and economic extent possible. One-storey houses, ground-floor flats, and flats with lifts must all be made available and suitable for the disabled person. Lift provision must be more generous and four-storey houses should always be supplied with lifts.

The basis for the provision of integration is not easy to define. A number of different possibilities exist and each must be tried out. It is a matter of trial and error and an attempt must be made to assess the success of each solution, and inevitably this will be a lengthy process, but a necessary one if we are ever to find the solution to integration. A technical solution is not in itself enough and a support service system has to be created in parallel. The assistance which the disabled person needs must be established, possibly in the form of municipal home-helps who visit the disabled once a day to dress or wash him, clean the accommodation or arrange the delivery of meals.

For the most severely disabled persons more detailed considerations will be necessary as frequent personal assistance is essential, particularly if the disabled person is totally immobile. For them the desirable housing type must surely be one near the centre of activity, the shops, public transport and suitable leisure pursuits. The planning of urban developments has usually tended to concentrate round the railway station or underground, the shops, cinemas and leisure activity centres. Further away are the denser housing developments and further away still are the single-family houses with a garden. In this last area shops and amenities tend to be scarce. For the immobile disabled person the distances involved in travelling to the centre will be great and they will understandably prefer to live near the city centre. In Denmark we have had the pleasure of being able to follow to a large extent the principles mentioned and architects and builders have tried hard to plan and erect buildings suitable for disabled persons. A special housing association was established in 1953 by the National Association of Cripples, specifically to provide improved housing for more severely disabled people and their families. Later this Association was followed by others in this field. The National Association of Cripples has seen as its principal object an attempt to improve the housing conditions of handicapped persons who, given a certain amount of care—but not so much as to require their living in a nursing home—can manage to remain independent provided they have a suitable dwelling and the possibility of obtaining prepared food, and assistance with cleaning, dressing and shopping. Such people were previously, as a result of the difficulties in obtaining care, referred to nursing homes.

As its first task the Building Society under the leadership

of its then chairman, the former Minister of State (Prime Minister) Viggo Kampmann, embarked upon the planning of a collective house for disabled people in Copenhagen. This building was the first of its kind in the world and there was but limited information and experience upon which to draw in connection with the arrangement and design of the apartments.

The focus of the idea of the collective house was the wish to enable the handicapped to lead a life as near normal as possible. The arrangement and layout of these flats had consequently to be carried out with this object in view. In addition there had to be ready access to personal catering, charring, shopping and individual support managed in the most convenient manner.

The total floor area of the collective house is 16,500 square metres, distributed over thirteen storeys. In all, the house contains 170 flats. All flats are arranged with special consideration for the demands which must necessarily be made when severely handicapped persons are to live in them. In order to avoid an institutional atmosphere in the building only about one-third of the flats are let out to handicapped people. The other tenants are able-bodied people who would like to make use of the extra facilities which the collective house contains. The majority of the flats are small—sixty of one room, thirty-one of two rooms and seventy-nine of three rooms (+ kitchen). They are all up to date as to equipment without being over-luxurious, and only a small minority have their own kitchen; the remainder have a kitchenette where lighter meals may be prepared. This solution to the kitchen problem must be viewed against the fact that the tenants have access to the restaurant of the collective house, which also, upon request, sees to the delivery of food and refreshment for parties, and also special diets. If one does not wish to dine in the restaurant itself, dinner may be sent up from the restaurant kitchen to the flat.

In the thirteenth storey of the collective house has been arranged—with considerable support from the National

Association against Polio—a special nursing home for fifteen to seventeen polio patients suffering from paralysis of the respiratory organs. The single polio patient lives in the nursing home itself, with a trained staff, easy access to medical aid, and the requisite technical aids and apparatus. Such patients (who normally live with their families) have had six of the ordinary flats of the collective house placed at their disposal. These flats are provided with special equipment and security measures and at night the patients can sleep and be under satisfactory attendance in a number of special rooms in the nursing home, where such relatives may also stay in cases of illness, or while their family is away on holiday. In the nursing home are also to be found sitting-rooms, a school-room, where respiratorily paralysed children are taught together with children from outside, roof gardens, and administrative offices. This nursing home is conducted as an independent unit, and quite apart from the administration of the collective house.

The house contains accommodation for disabled persons from all over Denmark, who receive tuition at a workshop located in the vicinity of the collective house. This accommodation is in the form of a 'college'. Other accommodation includes a youth pension, where a score of very severely handicapped young people share six large apartments. Each has a private furnished room in a single apartment for three or four young people who manage the apartment on their own. Help is provided for cleaning and the young people may in common with the other tenants of the house call in assistance from the nursing centre. This centre provides assistance to the individual tenant according to his need, and thanks to this feature, as well as to the dining facilities and the other collective assistance arrangements, some thirty people are now living in the collective house as ordinary tenants who in the absence of those services would have had to spend their lives in a nursing home.

For the severely handicapped there are obvious difficulties in finding a job in normal trade and industry. In order to contribute towards the solution of this problem so-called 'protected workshops' have been established in the collective house in Copenhagen. In these workshops the handicapped are offered an opportunity to utilize their working ability to supplement their invalid pension. The workshops have been moved to another location outside the collective house where room for expansion is possible.

In addition to the restaurant and central kitchen there is a number of well designed reception and banqueting rooms, which can be let to the tenants of the house for family gatherings and parties, which would be difficult, if not impossible, to organize in the comparatively small flats. Also, a number of guest rooms on the twelfth storey are available to the tenants. In the basement there is an up-to-date central laundry, hobby rooms and stores for perambulators and invalid and wheelchairs. From an underground garage system there is direct access to the lifts in the collective house without any changes of level. Like the doors at the main entrance of the house, the garage doors are equipped with automatic opening mechanisms. This also applies to the doors of the seven lifts in the house. Even severely handicapped persons may with comparative ease get to and from their flats by motor-car. On the ground floor a special playroom has been arranged for the children, and on the thirteenth storey is the roof garden to which all the tenants have access. The staff of the clearing service of the collective house undertake for normal hourly wages the task of keeping the tenants' flats in order. At the reception desk in the front hall parcels and goods are received and the doorman or receptionist who also attends to the telephone switchboard is able twenty-four hours of the day to connect up the tenants' extension telephones with nurses, cleaning service, restaurant, inspector, or with the main telephone networks outside the house. Tenants who by reason of their disability require assistance in dressing and personal needs may summon aid through the telephone from one of the nurses. Those who are unable themselves to go down to the restaurant for their meals may likewise make arrangements with the restaurant for service in the flat.

A 'day-centre' was established in the collective house about four years ago. Here disabled persons from the whole area can work and talk together with others discussing their problems. The cost of the building and its contents—some Dkr. 15,500,000 (£820,000)—was obtained by means of credit, and mortgage loans, together with government loans in conformity with the legislation in support of building operations up to 94 per cent of the building cost. The remaining 6 per cent of these costs was covered by the tenants' contributions in the form of deposits and various grants, primarily from the Society and Home for Physical Handicapped and the Cripples' Foundation. The Municipality of Copenhagen has to an extent paid the deposits of those disabled persons where their financial circumstances justified this.

The total rent has been equated with the operating expenses. For a reduction of the rent, a house-rent allowance is paid by the Municipality of Copenhagen, depending on the taxable income of the tenant. To invalids and the chronically ill the house-rent allowance is accorded in conformity with income, number of children and area of flat. Single invalid pensioners in one-room flats have their rent reduced to Dkr. 150 (£8) per month, corresponding to approximately 10–15 per cent of their monthly pension.

Twelve years have now passed since the collective house on Hans Knudsens Plads was established and this period has provided a wealth of experience both about the faults in the initial design of the building and about the planning and organization of the personal assistance system that has made it possible for more and more severely disabled tenants to live in the collective house. Based on the experience of Hans Knudsens Plads the Building Society has erected 1,100 flats in nine buildings, and a further eight buildings with about 900 flats are now in the planning stage. Negotiations are in progress regarding the establishment of five other buildings with 700 flats. Thus during the next five-year period it is expected that the Building Society will be operating about 3,000 flats.

Collective houses will be established in the bigger towns, and it is especially this task that the Cripples' Building Society has accepted. The Building Society has meanwhile also developed single-family houses with a garden suitable for severely disabled persons in the rural areas and at the moment there are twenty-five such houses being established each year. The rural areas offer few facilities for the disabled and suitable dwellings to rent are scarce so the Building Society's work in these areas is very necessary.

4

Holland's approach to residential care

A. KLAPWIG and W. P. BIJLEVELD

'Het Dorp' is one of several answers to the problem of providing a home and a way of life for a large number of severely disabled men and women in Holland. The following is intended as an explanation of the background, the philosophy and the principles that underlie this novel and unique experiment. Het Dorp is also a complex structure of human relationships which will be examined in some depth.

In the 1950s those working in the field of physical handicap became increasingly concerned at the growing and immense problems faced by the seriously handicapped who were unable to find an acceptable way of life, despite all traditional attempts at rehabilitation. Unlike those who have been successfully rehabilitated, these citizens remain permanent invalids. The cause of their disability included: cerebral palsy, spina bifida, serious congenital deformities of the limbs, serious poliomyelitis, muscular dystrophy, rheumatoid arthritis, multiple sclerosis, severe paraplegias and other major traumas.

It was not known then, nor is it known now, just how many permanently handicapped people there are in Holland. Therefore it will be extremely difficult to predict with any degree of accuracy how this number will develop in the future, particularly as we cannot anticipate what change will be brought about by new medical and ethical considerations in the future. And we must consider that the group with congenital malformations will probably be balanced by the following influences. First, if the development of early research on amnion fluid can improve our prenatal prediction, the incidence of handicapped birth could well diminish by an increasing proportion of pregnancy terminations. Second, a substantial improvement in pre-natal care, and in post-natal care of the premature infant, will increase the survival rate of handicapped infants.

In general it seems reasonable therefore to postulate that more people with a serious and multiple handicap will grow older and their number will increase as a result of modern techniques before, during and after birth, as a result of improved operative and anaesthetic techniques, as a result of new means of preventing or fighting infection and better methods of rehabilitation.

Naturally, care had always been provided for permanent invalids, especially by their parents who often did the job alone and unaided until they became old and infirm themselves, and had to face the often asked question, 'What will happen to our child when we are gone?' Or there was the rehabilitation centre, where the disabled had to stay without prospect of further improvement, and no hope of an acceptable way of life. And there were the nursing homes, nursing institutions and hospitals. But these institutes inevitably meant that the disabled patients were obliged to remain in bed, though they were not actually ill, but merely immobile and in need of personal assistance. And in some cases the further tragedy of the separation of husband and wife is brought about if one remains at home and the other is institutionalized.

In 1959 Dr Klapwig was appointed director of the Johanna Foundation in Arnhem, the first Dutch institute for non-adult physically handicapped and there was an opportunity to develop this foundation into a modern rehabilitation centre. It was felt to be unfair that a centre intended primarily for those who could be rehabilitated to the point of self-sufficiency had been established while there was still no solution for those more severely handicapped who could not be completely rehabilitated. It was, therefore, necessary to find a way to help severely disabled people to achieve optimal human development and optimal human happiness.

Those of us who are not handicapped and who live in a modern welfare state tend to take for granted several minimum comforts. All of us create our lives on the basis of the privacy of our own living quarters, the opportunity to work or at least to pursue useful occupations, recreation and relaxation, participation in cultural life, the opportunity to fulfil religious needs and a democratic right-of-say in our private and community lives. It was evident that the severely handicapped had precisely the same rights, but adapted to the special demands of their handicaps, and the idea of 'Het Dorp', which means simply 'The Village', was born. From the beginning, it was clear that such a village would have to fulfil certain essential requirements. First, it would have to be in the immediate vicinity of a rehabilitation centre or an institute that could offer sufficient rehabilitation facilities, not only because permanently disabled people need the best possible medical and paramedical treatment if they are to reach maximum achievement, but also because they must be able to profit from every new technical development, the adaptation of which could help them to improve their prospects. Furthermore, the village itself would then need to provide only minimum medical care, and could thus itself avoid becoming a medical institution.

Second, the village should be built as an integral part of a city and not as an isolated community. It could then help the handicapped to be integrated into the world of the able-bodied and to contribute to the integration of the handicapped and non-handicapped in our society. These two requirements, the presence of rehabilitation facilities and the situation in a city, could both be fulfilled in Arnhem. Adjacent to the Johanna Foundation and just between two districts of the city were about sixty-five acres of lovely open ground, an ideal setting for a community of 400 seriously handicapped people. Thanks to the positive reactions of the Netherlands population, enough money was raised to enable the village to be built, and thanks to both national and city governments, one of our modern laws could be adapted for the working expenses of the village.

The next step was a thorough study by a group of experts, and the construction of Het Dorp finally began in 1964. Supervision was by two professors of architecture, Messrs van der Broek and Bakema. The whole construction was finished in 1970, six years later. Ultimately the village will house nearly 400 handicapped inhabitants. To describe this new neighbourhood in Arnhem, it is necessary to refer to those minimum human comforts that are the basis on which we all tend to build our own lives.

The privacy of one's own living quarters

Every villager has his own private home. There is an entrance hall, bed-sitting room, simple cooking facilities, toilet, shower and wash-stand. The homes are not large, but each one provides complete privacy and each has its own front door with doorbell and letterbox. In addition to the general adaptations, each home has been built to meet the specific requirements of its inhabitants. Some front doors, for instance, can be opened and closed by the radio impulse provided by a small transmitter which the inhabitant carries on his electric wheelchair.

For each row of ten houses there is a covered street so that mobility, largely through electric wheelchairs, is guaranteed even in bad weather. Nine homes in each block of ten are inhabited by the handicapped. The tenth is for a non-uniformed, trained helper. There is a small community centre for every block of ten houses, where inhabitants in search of company can gather for discussions, card games, quiet evenings of talk and television-watching, and where meals can be served. Everyone in Het Dorp can choose exactly the degree of privacy or community living he wishes. The inhabitant of each house—and he only—decides what will go on within his own four walls, whether he will receive guests, when he will go to bed, and so on.

Some of our villagers are married; sometimes one, sometimes both partners of the marriage are handicapped. Couples live in twin houses converted into larger single homes. Each group of ten homes also has its own large kitchen for the preparation of more elaborate meals. Most of the inhabitants take their meals from the central kitchen and dine in their own houses or in the community centres. Personal care in the homes is provided by the trained resident helpers, who are assisted by other aides living in an apartment building in the central village square. Both indoor and outdoor streets and plazas have ordinary street names and each home has its own street number. Mail is delivered to the doors, as it is everywhere in Arnhem. Inhabitants with telephones are listed by their own names in the Arnhem directory.

Work or other occupation

A few inhabitants are employed outside the village, in Arnhem, and reach their work by special transport; 40 per cent of the villagers work in Het Dorp's sheltered workshops where their employment may be either clerical or manual labour. Het Dorp produces, for instance, toys, clothing and ceramics, and it prints and binds braille books, and tapes 'talking books' for the blind. Inhabitants have priority for employment in Het Dorp's own shops. Villagers who are not able to work under the new law on sheltered workshops find opportunity for useful and purposeful activities in specially built areas within the village.

Recreation, relaxation and cultural life

In addition to being able to relax in their own homes or community centres, villagers can make use of a wide range of other facilities: free access to Arnhem is available, including theatre, cinema, concert-hall, and museums. Where public transport is not suitable, villagers use Het Dorp's own buses, which are specially adapted for wheelchairs. On the central village square there is a religious and cultural centre with its own theatre. The restaurant with its open-air terrace provides ample space for large gatherings and for dinners and refreshments with villagers or other Arnhem citizens. The large gymnasium is used mostly for indoor sports activities such as table tennis and archery. A library is available.

The opportunity to fulfil religious needs

Villagers go to their churches in Arnhem, if they are able. If not, they attend services in their own church in the village which has been built and is used by all denominations.

Finally, most important is the democratic right of each villager to express his point of view about his personal life and his membership of the community and its management. For years the seriously handicapped individual has had little or no opportunity to participate actively in everyday community life, which is, after all, structured to meet the requirements of the able-bodied. Limited mobility, often difficult speech and the well-intentioned but domineering bossiness of non-handicapped fellow citizens all contribute to the problem. Extreme examples are nursing institutes where management, doctors and nursing staffs are often unavoidably forced to make the decisions. After years in such situations, handicapped people often allow themselves to be pampered, giving in to the supremacy of the able-bodied.

As Het Dorp and the experiment developed, serious consideration was given to finding ways in which disabled villagers could be given opportunities for participation and the right to self-expression in government within the village. Democracy in the village is essentially a two-sided thing. On the one hand it is concerned with the need to involve the inhabitants in the decisions and policies that influence the organization and its environment. On the other hand, it is also necessary that the organizational requirements are reflected in the decision-making of the residents. Such a process demands a mutual exchange of ideas made possible by the establishment of a series of councils, committees and study groups forming a democratic structure of representation in which majority and minority voices can be heard alongside the views of those who are charged with the duty of care.

In 1963 forty future villagers were invited to a special conference to discuss the concept of the village, the design of the buildings, and a number of other aspects of the village in the future. Following this conference a committee of the six leading handicapped members of the conference—and known locally as 'the Parliament'—was appointed, meeting every six weeks in Arnhem to discuss any new problems regarding the village. It is interesting to note that nearly all the suggestions made by this committee were carried out. There is now a very democratic electoral system. Every thirty inhabitants, or three groups of ten homes, form a district and elect one representative to the Village Council. Two of its members are chosen by the Council, to become members of the Executive Board of the 'Het Dorp' Foundation. Self-responsibility throughout the village has been a feature of village life wherever possible. Recreational and cultural activities are organized by a citizens' commission which is appointed by the Council, and the Commission manages its own budget. Some villagers, especially those who have a long period of institutional life behind them, have not yet become used to their new-found freedom and responsibility. Adaptation involves a process of growth.

Study or working groups have also been employed. One such group of residents is currently working on the issue of sexual relationships for the benefit of other residents. Other groups work from time to time to consider other issues and where necessary staff and residents sit together in these groups.

Gratifying, even though it might have been expected, was the discovery that a handicapped person has as much managerial ability as the able-bodied. The non-handicapped management and staff of Het Dorp have found it quite easy to lay all manner of problems before the Village Council and its sub-committee which are responsible for the village's recreational activities, the production of the village journal, *The Village Key*, and the budgets that relate to these activities.

To return for a moment to the two essential requirements of such a village that have already been mentioned, Het Dorp is adjacent to the Johanna Foundation rehabilitation centre, in fact just across a secondary road. Villagers receive there the necessary medical and nearly all paramedical treatment, which is primarily physical and occupational therapy. X-ray, laboratory and dental departments of the centre are also open to villagers. The village, like all Dutch communities, has a 'neighbourhood centre' and here the general practioner is to be found and three qualified nurses are in residence to advise and, where necessary, help the resident assistants and their aides.

To fulfil the second requirement, Het Dorp is essentially an integral part of the city of Arnhem, and operates as a normal city district.

Surrounding the central village square are the restaurant, the Automobile Club building (where a specialized service in tours for the handicapped is beginning to take form), the post office (run by villagers), a petrol station, a beauty parlour and hairdresser, a supermarket, a library and a religious-cultural centre. These are all regarded as vital and essential village services and they provide employment to villagers. More important, they are additionally points of integration and contact that tie Het Dorp to the surrounding Arnhem districts. Here voluntary relationships are formed between the handicapped and the able-bodied, among *equals*, whose new ties, one with the other, give life a dimension which, if not new, is one which has been long forgotten.

It is necessary to consider the basis on which villagers were selected. From the very beginning it was felt that it was essential to accept in Het Dorp only those disabled people who could create and maintain a satisfactory life in the village, who would not be in a position to do so outside it. The following basic criteria were defined as objectives for the village:

(1) It is, in principle, intended for the handicapped of all ages. In reality, however, handicapped young people are usually still undergoing a process of rehabilitation until their eighteenth or twentieth birthday and the handicapped in their sixties often prefer to be placed in homes for the aged.

(2) The village prefers to accept only the handicapped who have achieved a maximum of rehabilitation before arrival, but in this connection the age of the candidate and the nature of his handicap must be taken fully into consideration.

(3) It was not established for the mentally handicapped, since its community can do little to help them. In this context one is concerned less with the intelligence quotient of the candidate than with his degree of social competence and whether he can provide a positive contribution to the community and himself profit from the association.

(4) Het Dorp is not intended for those whose handicap is limited to the sensory organs, but those with a motor handicap plus a sensory disability will qualify for admission.

(5) The severity of the handicap is not of course a deciding factor for admission to Het Dorp since both general and individual facilities are adapted and specifically designed to cater for severe handicap and the achievement of the most complete life possible, within the limits of the handicap and the ingenuity of the planners.

In selecting residents, Het Dorp strives first of all to serve the interests of the candidate. The village is not always the right solution and a candidate might be better served outside the village. Alternative solutions will always be considered with an eye to achieving the greatest possible degree of development for the handicapped person in question. The selection committee consists of experts from Het Dorp itself, such as a rehabilitation doctor, a public health expert, a social worker, a psychologist and others more acquainted with the special problems of the candidate himself. These include regional or institutional health authorities, social workers, vocational specialists and so forth.

To date nearly 1,300 candidates have been considered. Many have been advised to go to rehabilitation centres and after treatment they have often been able to return to their home-towns and a reasonably normal life in suitably adapted homes. Some candidates were simply not suited to community life; others needed the care of institutions for the mentally handicapped.

Whatever 'Het Dorp' may be it is certainly not a kind of 'heaven upon earth'. Far from it. It is a typically earthly community with typically human shortcomings, in which the residents have the usual range of problems. Many visitors, both professional and casual, who come to the village for the first time, often ask if there is not an objection to such a concentration of so many handicapped in one location.

Economic motives

If we are quite serious about the individual happiness of a severely handicapped fellow man we should accept that we must provide such a person with the greatest opportunities for happiness and a full life; yet this would be economically impossible for a small group. We would have to compromise with the ideal and the ideal is the target we have set. With a larger number of people the common overhead costs will be reduced in such a way that the ideal indeed can be realized. Experience so far suggests that the present number of 400 severely handicapped people is sufficient to provide ample economic justification for the price we have to pay, a price often lower than that of other solutions, such as the nursing home.

Community motives

Were we successful in integrating a small number of severely handicapped people in an ordinary and conventional community, there would be a probability that they would not be able to play an active and democratic role in that community, largely because it would not have been organized to make this possible. In the village this aspect has been successful. The 'Parliament' and the village community committee give a fair chance for the development of resident participation, even for the most severely handicapped residents. This is of greatest importance to the maintenance of self-respect, one of our most fundamental human dignities.

One cannot pretend that there are no problems in this new district of Arnhem. They are a consequence of the fact that the inhabitants are severely handicapped. Although modern rehabilitation has made great achievements, it is still very difficult to find appropriate work for all the disabled inhabitants. This of course is understandable in view of the problems of employing people with a serious motor malfunction. A degree (which is an important asset for an able-bodied job-hunter) will, on the other hand, be of little importance to the severely handicapped youngster who may never be able to find a job in which his degree can be used, and encouragement to obtain academic qualifications should not be forced. Better vocational evaluation methods are necessary. Doctors of rehabilitation, psychologists and vocational specialists must have the courage to give an early prognosis of the function that the handicapped youngster can fulfil in future. Improved special educational and assessment methods for them are necessary if we are to improve our assessment services. On the other hand, in educating the handicapped youth, we must once and for all banish the myth that working solely for financial gain can alone provide enjoyment and a sense of purpose. We have to convince them that labour or employment without such reward can and does provide a purposeful meaning in life.

In this respect we shall have to fight against the current images in our society that regard unrewarded labour and employment as being less desirable than labour which has a productive function.

Integration of the disabled in a normal society is another problem. The process has two faces. The first demands that we prepare the handicapped to live in and with a society whose construction seldom provides for their wishes. Rehabilitation of youngsters can be positively introduced by means of social and socio-cultural activity, especially by clubs for handicapped and able-bodied young people. On the other hand the non-handicapped youth will have to be educated in school and after to live with the handicapped and to understand their problems. We have already started to do this in Holland, especially among our youth in schools and our experience so far in this connection has been exceptionally good. Perhaps the issue should be seen the other way round. Those who are not handicapped usually consider their attitude and their way of life to be an example for those who are handicapped.

Integration in the outside community may be a slow process. A prerequisite for the village residents is their ability to integrate within the village environment and, having achieved this, to attract Arnhem and its population to the village itself. This has been achieved in some measure. Residents have many family contacts in the local city. The village's amenities are used by able-bodied locals just as Arnhem's shopping and leisure or cultural amenities are available to the villagers. Even a recent political tour included Het Dorp in its itinerary. The village has produced an exciting example for us all of a new democratic and self-help approach to integration.

Until recently, housing in the village was financed by special obligatory financial deductions from salary or private income. Soon a new law for the payment of housing rents will be introduced and with it will come the end of the obligatory deduction. The decision was taken by the inhabitants of the village at a special meeting. By voting 350 for and 2 against they decided to introduce the following system: each inhabitant with an adequate income can retain Fl. 200 (£137.50) each month. Those receiving more than Fl. 200 pay 50 per cent of the excess to the community fund. The costs of living are partially paid by this fund. Those who receive no payment, or do not have an income, get money from this community fund. One has to assume that each inhabitant is willing to help the other within his ability. And this is the beginning of mutual self-help. One must wonder how many other cities or villages in the world have communities willing to live together in this way. It is clearly noticeable in and around the village that integration is advancing, perhaps as a result of the many opportunities for mutual respect between handicapped and able-bodied.

Technical aids

So severely handicapped are some of the village residents that for them the only sensible solution lies in the provision of suitable technical aids. In 1970 a new foundation called 'Adaptationcentre' was established at Johanna Stichting which Het Dorp had created to promote research in and manufacture of technical aids. There have already been some promising results from the work of this foundation and high expectations are held for the future of this new centre.

Much work needs to be done in this field on a national and international basis and we should combine our research if we are to gain the most efficient results. The more progress that can be made in this way the greater will be the fulfilment of the lives of the many severely handicapped the world over.

The village must be seen as an experiment, perhaps as a successful experiment, and not the only solution for the problems of all physically handicapped people. It is intended to be complementary to a number of other solutions to the living problems of the handicapped. Disability is manifest in several ways and each may have several solutions. But probably only one will provide that quality and fullness of life the opportunity to achieve which we are all seeking in our own ways to make available to the disabled person.

The following basic management rules must apply to the whole field of rehabilitation of the handicapped: before any measure is proposed for an individual an assessment in detail has to be made by a team of medical, social, educational and vocational experts. Only then will proper information be provided about the possibilities *and* the impossibilities for the person involved. And such an assessment must be undertaken at the very beginning of disability or illness. Only after this assessment can long-term rehabilitation be planned. It is obvious that during this period the rehabilitation will be a major consideration. Another important consideration will be the provision of proper housing for the disabled person and his family and this should offer the maximum independence and integration consistent with the limitations of the handicap involved.

Het Dorp wishes to encourage both itself and others never to settle for half-measures or partial solutions to human problems. And to commend to the world of care for the handicapped, the Bible's Golden Rule: 'Whatsoever you would that men should do to you, do you even so to them.'

A picture of 'Het Dorp' would not be complete without some statistical and economic background. In March 1971 the total number of inhabitants of the village was 387 disabled and 8 able-bodied, of whom 277 were female, and 168 were male; included in this number are 37 couples (twenty-nine couples both partners disabled and eight couples with one partner disabled). The village has a total capacity for 405 residents. Hot meals are provided by a central kitchen. Attendants, known as *dogelas*, look after the households of the inhabitants where the latter cannot do this themselves. Some inhabitants, although they need the protection of the village, are able to care for the household and cater for themselves. For this reason a building for self-sufficient married couples and a few single persons has been provided where staff do only the personal nursing.

Some flats are occupied by couples, of whom one partner is able-bodied. This means that the total capacity has decreased to 400 physically handicapped residents leaving accommodation for a further thirteen people. The selection of these thirteen residents has taken place and they will soon move into the village. Surprisingly the number of females is greater than the number of males. Possibly a disabled man needs the protection of the village less than a disabled woman, because the handicapped man—in contrast with the woman—can be more easily cared for with the support of the family.

The village has provided a real opportunity for marriage and only in exceptional cases had a person married before the handicap occured. At the moment ten resident applications have been made for accommodation of this type and there is the possibility of creating sixty more dwelling-quarters for couples by combining two single dwellings. Such combinations of course depend on the co-operation of the single persons living in the units concerned. If a person wants to marry he is put on a waiting list, if at the time no accommodation is available.

The number of males and females distributed by age are shown in Table 4.1.

TABLE 4.1: *Numbers of males and females distributed by age*

Age	*Total*	*Men*	*Women*
Over 65	8	1	7
between 60–65	19	7	12
55–60	27	9	18
50–55	41	15	26
45–50	47	21	26
40–45	44	16	28
35–40	41	13	28
30–35	48	20	28
25–30	57	35	22
20–25	54	24	30
20	1	1	—

From the totals in Table 4.1 it appears that the age pyramid gives a reasonably normal picture. The number in the lower age brackets is higher than in the higher age range.

Diagnoses

Cerebral palsy 98
Multiple sclerosis 50
Muscular dystrophy 47
Polio 28
Rheumatism 27
Spina bifida 27
Encephalopathy on traumatic or operative base 23
Friedreich's ataxia 13
Congenital malformations 7
Osteogenesis imperfecta 6
Other somatic diseases 5
Arthogryposis 4
Bechterew disease 3
Parkinson's disease 3
Still's disease 3
Syringomyelia 3
Congenital luxation of the hips 3
Idiopathic kyphoscoliosis 3
Morquio disease 2
Chondrodystrophy 2
Haemophilia 1
Myositis ossificans 1
Sclerodermia 1
Coxitis tuberculosa 1
Spastic spinal paraplegia 1
Epilepsy 1
Normal 8

The survey shows that the cerebral palsy group is by far the largest, with muscular dystrophy and multiple sclerosis a close second. This might suggest that in Holland alternative nursing facilities are not readily available. Of a total of 387 residents, 154 or approximately 40 per cent suffer from a progressive illness. This percentage is high and involves a number of specific problems. Sooner or later such a resident will require care twenty-four hours a day and it must be considered whether that person, for his or her own sake, should remain in the village or be transferred to a twenty-four hours a day nursing home.

It will be easily understood that if a disabled person comes to the village knowing in advance that as a consequence of his progressive illness he will have to leave the village some time in the future, this fact will have some psychological effect on his attitude, on his social adaptation and on his ability to integrate in the village. It is felt that in such cases the principle of personal free choice should operate. This could imply that, in the future we might have to organize a twenty-four hours a day nursing service, but this is at the moment still being studied. So far it has been possible to supply the necessary nursing help in the residents' own living quarters.

Activities during the day

Residents are encouraged to find employment if they are are capable of work outside the village. There is regular contact with the Labour Exchange and transport is provided. For those residents for whom such possibilities are not available, employment and occupation is provided in the village. Here there is a workshop, divided into two departments; the manual labour department and the 'mental' labour department. But only a small number of the resident population is able to work in the workshop because the Dutch government demands one-third of normal productivity before admission is granted. This means that large numbers of the residents are obliged to seek alternative daytime occupation when they are not able to work. Dutch law provides subsidies for such an occupation project and the village has on this basis been able to organize a Recreation Centre. Table 4.2 shows the number of residents who are employed in the various departments.

TABLE 4.2: *Number of residents employed*

Employment	*Number*
A. Working in ordinary competitive employment situated outside the village, including the municipal sheltered workshop *Presikhaaf*	18
Working on own account as watchmakers, interpreters and readers	5
Total	23

TABLE 4.2 *cont.*	*Employment*	*Number*
	Being employed by the village in:	
	Community service (wheelchair repair, carpenter's yard and telephone service)	7
	Secretarial (including mail delivery)	3
	Post Office	2
	Telephone service workshop	2
	Public Library	2
	Secretariat Village Council	2
	Medical centre	1
	Kiosk restaurant De Sleutel (The Key)	5
	ITBON (Scientific observation of flora and fauna around the village)	1
	Total	25
B.	Sheltered workshop *Hengemunde:*	
	(i) Manual labour	
	Ready-made clothing	12
	Toys	6
	Pottery	8
	Assembling	31
	Packing	30
	Total	87
	(ii) Mental labour	
	Reading books for the blind	32
	Typewriting	13
	Reading books on tape for the blind	2
	Colour photographs	1
	Administration	10
	Total	58
C.	Visitors' Recreation Centre (handicrafts etc.)	72
	Working as member of committee, such as Editorial Committee, Recreation Committee	13
	Total	85
	Total of all employment capacities	278

This, out of the total of 387 residents, leaves 109 residents with no specific or regular work. Of these a number arrived only a few months ago and it is evident that most of the inhabitants need quite a long time for adaptation before they are able to spend a meaningful day. In addition a number of residents undertake certain training courses or hobbies. There remains nevertheless a considerable number who spend the day as a consequence of their severe handicap in complete passivity.

Attempts are now being made in co-operation with the Dutch government to extend the Recreation Centre in such a manner that residents of the village together with the local people living in Arnhem can work and play together. If this plan succeeds, integration will improve in a significant way and for the severely disabled resident greater possibilities will be provided.

Investments

Capital investments for the development were as shown in Table 4.3.

TABLE 4.3: *Development capital investment*

Investment	£
Purchase of building site	545,866
Layout of roads, grounds etc.	229,899
Layout of gardens	24,915
Buildings and installations	2,703,285
Inventories	215,175
Initial costs	192,525
Cash in bank on hand of subsidiary foundations	106,455
Total	£4,018,120

In response to a twenty-four hour radio and television marathon appeal in 1962 the capital sum of £2,944,507 was raised, including interest and legacies. The comparison of the £3,719,139 investment with the capital of the foundation (£2,944,507) indicates that funds had to be borrowed in the open market to the extent of £1,132,502. The figures show that £3,719,139 was invested in purchasing the building site, layout of the roads, gardens, buildings, installation and inventories, and that the average investment per resident amounted to £9,173.

Considering that the investment per bed place in a general hospital during construction is approximately £14,156 and that the average investment amounts to £10,192 per bed in a nursing home built at the same time, the construction was relatively inexpensive. Those who are interested in the architectural considerations should read the article on the village by Selwyn Goldsmith in the *Architectural Review* of April 1971.

The structure of the village has a superior Holding Foundation with two inferior foundations concerned with 'Operation' and 'Industry'. The village as Holding Foundation lets the buildings and site where the residents work to the 'Industry' foundation and all other building site to the 'Operation' foundation. The sheltered workshop is run in accordance with the Law on Sheltered Workshops. This law requires that the state subsidizes the wages, including social support for the disabled employees to a certain maximum, on condition that the accounting and organization remains separated from the rest of the village. All operational costs except those of the 'Industry' foundation are born by the 'Operation' foundation. An inhabitant pays boarding terms of £6·87 per day in addition to which a charge of £1·82 per day for the able-bodied partner of a disabled tenant is made. At the moment this cost is paid through application of the General Assistance Law. The Special Health Insurance will apply to the village from 1 January 1971 when the cost will be raised to approximately £7·30 per day as a result of the inclusion in this figure of the costs of the rehabilitation physicians and of supplying paramedical therapies, medicament and laboratory services.

TABLE 4.4: *Staff occupations and numbers*

Occupation		*Number*
Nursing care department:		
Office manager and assistant		2
Attendants		200
District attendants		5
Linen-room		3
District nurses		5
Physicians		1
Others		3
Staff-block matron and assistant		2
Household attendants		4
Staff training:		
Lady instructors		5
Pastor		1
	Total	231
Civil department:		
Office manager and assistant		2
Technical service		12
Wheelchair repair		12
External traffic		6
Internal traffic and store		6
Canteen		3
Cleaning service		17
Telephone service		7
Adaptation section		4
	Total	69
Staff matters		3
Management-secretariat (reception, mail department, purchase department)		15
Central kitchen		14
Administration		13
Recreation and recreation centre		7
Social department		2
	Total	54
Total number of staff		354

Staff

The staff is made up as shown in Table 4.4.

The personal and domestic care of the 400 residents is undertaken by 200 attendants in the ratio of 1 to 2. The training facilities provided for in the village have official recognition.

Conclusions: Community care for the severely physically handicapped

DEREK LANCASTER-GAYE

Two issues arise repeatedly in the consideration of the different approaches to residential care to be found in Great Britain, Holland, Denmark and Sweden. These issues are concerned with the problems of integration in the community and with the need for work, and a constructive or purposeful occupation, and it is appropriate that they should be examined here in greater detail.

It is evident that each country has been influenced to a greater or lesser extent in the way it has sought to accommodate physically disabled by the intention to secure some sort of integration of the disabled with the community in which they are to live. In Great Britain, for example, the tendency to establish small communities of forty or fifty disabled people in rural areas, a tendency which was itself the result of economic considerations rather than social realities, has given way to the more practical alternative of developing smaller communities still in urban housing areas where residents have direct access to local shopping facilities and community amenities. Denmark's approach has, if anything, been more directly associated with the need to integrate its disabled by establishing mixed housing in an urban area in which disabled and able-bodied residents live alongside each other with a carefully controlled maximum limit on the numbers in each category. After ten years it can be seen that this approach has not been unsuccessful though it is interesting to speculate what would have been the position had there not during this time been an acute housing shortage, bearing in mind that the 'collective house' in which they live and which also accommodates a nursing home for the very severely disabled is both known and seen locally to be what it is, a solution to the housing problems of the handicapped.

Sweden's Fokus organisation has achieved much the same end result as that found in Denmark, but by allocating only a limited number of specially designed dwellings throughout large housing estate areas and supported by non-residential services, they have been able to secure a more subtle integration within the normal community. Holland, on the other hand, has perhaps seen integration as something rather different and recognizing the quite considerable problems of circulation and mobility which must surely be fundamental to effective integration have sought to provide accommodation on a large scale in an area in which the total environment has been designed with its residents in mind. Whilst few would attempt to deny that its 400 residents, all of whom are severely physically disabled, are both happy and have a full and worthwhile existence some few hundred yards from the centre of a large urban population, the extent to which they have been able to achieve what we understand by integration is open to question.

In some measure the issue seems to turn upon just what we understand by 'integration with the community'. Is this a state of equality in which the disabled and able-bodied have equal opportunities to make important day to day decisions and opportunities of choice, a choice of where to go and how to get there, of who to visit and who to invite? Or is it a state in which all have equal rights to privacy, or such privacy as the normal community is able to offer in the world of today. Yet again does integration have something to do with security, of feeling part of something larger, of a community that may bring with it experiences of friendship and of the constructive contributions to a community that in their turn relate to something as simple as human dignity?

The disabled are often referred to as a 'minority group',

yet with the possible exception of the ethnic non-white issues, the disabled are to be found amongst both majority and minority groups alike. To classify them separately in this way not only appears to defy the dictates of logic but also to perpetuate the problems of facilitating both their acceptance by society and their ability to live in it.

Perhaps one of the more cogent approaches to the issue is to consider the opposite to integration, that of isolation or a state of separation from the community. This is a state that we are, of course, seeking to reverse and it is one brought about by a lack of contact with the community and the whole understanding of integration must turn on the provision of contact. Lack of contact is brought about by the presence of architectural barriers within the community, by an almost total lack of transportation in a situation in which contact and mobility are almost synonymous and by a lack of understanding of the problems of the disabled by the community at large.

Independence was a quality clearly sought in each of the countries whose systems of residential care were examined. It is a relative quality of life which is not necessarily the same thing as integration and was seen to be achieved in a situation where the environment was itself cut off from the rest of the community. Independence is also an effective aid towards keeping the economy within reasonable bounds and is an attraction to the staff who have to work in a care setting. In any event, community living cannot be seen to provide a real degree of independence for the disabled without the other factors now being considered.

If we accept that an awareness of the disabled and an understanding of their problems is an essential ingredient to successful integration then it must follow that the siting of accommodation for the disabled must allow adequate contact with the rest of the community, whether urban or rural, and whether the disabled are able to mix with the community or whether in cases of severe physical disability the community has to come to them. Unfortunately, public awareness of socially disadvantaged groups is a slow process and it is interesting to note that in each of the four countries involved in this review this awareness has eventually gone hand in hand with some form of legislation. In Denmark this legislation was provided soon after the last war, and the motivation behind the special provisions made for the disabled has its roots now in a social rather than a legal conscience. Integration is a state that cannot be forced either upon the disabled, who might not wish to be integrated as the planners would have it, or upon the community and there would appear to be no set formula capable of application to the many variables seen to exist in the field of residential care of the disabled and the wide ranges of disability involved. And both must be prepared for it, a process which we have already seen can be and usually is a slow one.

For the majority of the severely disabled, their disability also means immobility when dependent upon conventional means of transportation. The average urban environment has not yet come to terms with motorized wheelchairs and with members of the community who cannot walk even the shortest distance. Shops, cinemas and work places remain inaccessible to the majority in all but the most recent urban developments. The problem is seen very much as one of environmental planning geared to locate housing for the disabled as an integral unit in which its occupant has, within the limitations of his handicap, the same contacts and the same opportunities as his able-bodied fellows. It is in some measure essentially an architectural and environmental planning problem. Perhaps less so for the more severely handicapped whose main requirement is continuous care in a residential setting and where the issues at stake are the extent to which the residents of such centres can be located within the community as a group and the extent to which that community will be willing to accept their arrival and their limited participation in community affairs. This last point is perhaps the basis for the difference in the approach to care in the United Kingdom and on the Continent.

And does integration work? In each of the countries

examined, claims are made that it does. Certainly there is evidence to support this though in the final analysis it is the community and the disabled who live in that community who can assert that this is so. And some credit must go to those voluntary agencies whose pressures and advice have in some measure influenced the public opinion and architectural planning that has provided the basis on which successful integration has been able to take place, especially in the Scandinavian countries.

The second issue with which we must be concerned is that of work and the role it plays in the life of a severely disabled person. We live in an age when leisure is gaining increasing importance and it is not unreasonable to question whether in view of the increasing problems related to the provision of work for those who cannot compete in open industry we should not seek to provide some alternative, be it cultural or leisure. With varying degrees of intensity, facilities for work are provided in each of the four countries. In Great Britain the vast majority of the residents in the Spastics Society's centres, though severely disabled, attended day work centres the majority of which were located in the residential centre or were provided specially for them nearby. There, it seemed, the basis was that the provision of work facilities, generally operated on industrial sub-contract lines, on a five days a week system was the natural approach to the issue. Certainly there was evidence to suggest that the disabled themselves, with only few exceptions, wished to work within the limits of their ability. And similar conclusions may be drawn from the experiences of Holland, Denmark, and Sweden.

Work is after all a fundamental life style and the imposition of this style upon disabled persons by society generally would seem to be quite natural. Reducing the motivation behind this life style to quite basic proportions, we work to enable us to live by the product of our work. It is an entirely economic philosophy. We have the ability to opt out if we do not accept this philosophy and if we are able to survive whilst doing so. Most modern social states see that we do survive even in these circumstances. As for the able-bodied so for the disabled. They too can opt out but one is bound to question whether the two sets of circumstances are strictly comparable. We are concerned with people whose productivity, in general terms, will be one-third or even substantially less than that of his able-bodied counterpart. How much of an act is the work in which he engages and how much satisfaction does he derive from striving for an end product which will seldom disclose the degree of effort that he has put into its production.

To most of us, work is seen as an external measure of achievement and one directly related to capacity and effort. The greater the achievement the greater becomes the status of the achiever. For the disabled to whom work of any sort is a material challenge, the opportunity to work and by so doing to achieve at least part of that sense of status within the community is seen as essential and the financial return is almost certainly of less significance than the ability to make some constructive contribution to society and to be seen to be making that contribution.

Of course, 'going to work' is a part of normal living, a contrast to that other part of our lives spent at home in a domestic environment free of the discipline and urgency of the factory or office. It is not only a normal experience but one which can and usually does bring with it new contacts, new friendships and stimulations not to be found in the more protective setting of home. It is a setting in which survival, independence and mutual help with other disabled persons are paramount. Of course we are right in seeking to make such work facilities available. But at the same time cultural or leisure activities should be made available as an alternative for those who by virtue of their handicap wish to exercise their right of choice.

The payments made to disabled workers in sheltered conditions, especially to those more severely handicapped whose output was on a quite modest scale, varied considerably from country to country. In some cases the size of the payment was restricted by the limited funds available.

In other cases limitations were imposed by the regulations in force governing the payment of special social security benefits. Generally, however, it was felt essential where workers whose widely varying handicaps resulted in an equally wide range of abilities and productivity for rewards not to be based on productivity but related more to effort where this was capable of assessment. Financial incentives were, however, possible where the ability of the workers showed no great variation and where one, by paying these incentives, would not be placing a premium on minimal handicap.

Whether these outlooks will change in the future when the pursuit of leisure plays an increasingly important role remains to be seen. The study of leisure and recreation for the disabled is an important field about which as yet little has been written and it is encouraging to be able to record the fact that the International Cerebral Palsy Society has now established a special Sports and Leisure Group whose function will be to look at this field, to disseminate information and to encourage exchanges.

Part Two

Sex, Marriage and the Heavily Handicapped Spastic

Introduction: Personal relationships and the heavily handicapped spastic person

JAMES A. LORING

During an age when sexual attitudes are becoming liberalized, there is a danger that something akin to a sexual apartheid will be created for the handicapped, with one set of rules for them and another for the able-bodied.

Human concepts of marriage and sexual relationships are essential parts of cultural patterns. The majority pattern in Western Europe and America is Christian with monogamy and sex-within-marriage as a public norm. There is very little quantitative evidence as to the extent to which these norms have been observed in the past, but the topic has created some academic interest, particularly during the last two decades, and studies of sexual behaviour of groups and evidence of aberration from accepted public norms have appeared in the literature. The Kinsey Reports on sexual behaviour in the human male and the human female have produced important evidence, although the structuring of the survey is zoological.

It would be difficult to list all the points of the Kinsey Reports which are particularly relevant to the situation of the handicapped, but amongst those that are particularly relevant are two. First, the immense variety in the extent of sexual outlet in all its forms in the human male and female, and second, the quantitative evidence of the extent to which deviations from the public norm (pre-marital and extra-marital intercourse, homosexuality, etc.) are contained in the Kinsey samples. Whether or not the Kinsey samples and method are accepted, the findings are at least sufficient to liberalize the intellectual standpoint of the more thoughtful of the orthodox.

If average sexual outlet in the human male varies from twice a month to twenty times a week—variation which apparently does not exist in animal species—then it would be sensible to assume that a similar variation exists amongst the handicapped and to anticipate some problems that needs of that order create. It is no longer sensible to believe that particular types of sexual behaviour are always expressions of psychosis or neurosis. More often they are expressions of what is biologically basic in anthropoid behaviour. Many of the complications observable in sexual histories are the result of society's reactions when it obtains knowledge of an individual's behaviour or the individual's fear of how society would react if he were so discovered. If, for example, the warden of a residential centre for the handicapped were to accept the basic sexual normality of his residents, it would follow that he would be confronted with a situation in which the male residents under the age of thirty would, on average, require three sexual outlets a week, and residents up to the age of eighty-five would require 2·75 outlets per week (average); if they were not handicapped, 75 per cent of his residents would have at least two sources of sexual gratification.

The way in which this situation is dealt with depends to a great extent upon the warden's personal views on sexual problems, and on his own sex patterns. The variation in attitude is wide-ranging from the prohibitive to the collusive. These are mere random thoughts on the subject of sex, and we must now proceed to the subject of marriage.

It is not sensible to discuss the subject of marriage of spastic couples without first accepting that the degree of physical handicap varies very considerably amongst spastics, ranging from the mildly handicapped spastic who is coping quite well in the community to the grossly handicapped spastic who requires total residential care. There is also the difference in range of intelligence which is so often forgotten but which is very important indeed. Many of the problems that arise in this area do not stem from cerebral palsy but rather from the fact that a significant percentage of the cerebral palsied are, in fact, in the sub-normal ranges, and marriage for these people even if they had no physical handicap would in itself present gross social problems.

Seminars and discussion groups produce a certain amount of anecdotal material about the marriage of spastics and it has been concerned mostly with the reaction of persons in charge of spastics to the prospects of their charges' marrying. It is worth recording that the majority of the cerebral palsied have an inalienable legal and moral right to marriage and it is also worth recording that parents of ordinary children are notorious for their inclination to intervene in the sexual and marital affairs of their young. Wardens of centres and homes and social workers are similarly concerned.

Complex problems arise when spastic people are in residential care. Emotional and sexual relationships form quite readily but in a great many cases ordinary physical manifestations are impeded by physical handicap. It is extraordinarily difficult to make love satisfactorily if both lovers are in wheelchairs. It is equally difficult for them to find places in a residential establishment where they can be alone.

How far should the staff of a residential centre be concerned in matters of this sort? Should their concern take the form of prohibitive intervention or of collusive intervention? Prohibitive intervention presents one range of problems which could claim as their backing conventional nineteenth-century sex morality and, although interventions of this sort will be resisted, they are for many 'on the side of the angels'. It is not suggested that the prohibitive attitude should be accepted, merely that given our immediate sexual antecedents, it is not difficult to obtain some acceptance.

The collusive intervention is in many ways the more interesting and more problematical. It presents itself in a number of situations: where, for example, the two handicapped people are emotionally or sexually attracted and wish to make love but not necessarily to have intercourse, and in the situation where the two handicapped people, perhaps claiming their intention to marry, wish to have pre-marital intercourse.

Given the contemporary attitude towards sex, two handicapped people could logically claim the rights and privileges of their unhandicapped brothers and sisters, and the great problem is to what extent should the staff of residential centres help them to achieve this and to what extent is it proper for us, who supervise the staff, to suggest that they should suppress their own moral principles in this matter.

These are just some of the problems in the area of sexuality facing the disabled and perhaps those who are closely concerned with their care. What are the views of the disabled themselves about their sexual relationships and what does society think about it all? Society does, of course, have more than one point of view. If it attributes normal rights and opportunities in this field to the severely disabled, what are we and what should we be doing to extend normal and purposeful sex education to the young disabled? To what extent can and should we provide opportunity for those who cannot obtain it unaided, and having provided it how far should we go in offering practical and technical aid in the sex act itself? And if society does not approve of these steps, how can we educate it to a more human point of view?

These points are treated in some depth in the following pages by both the disabled themselves and by the professionals. The views expressed are both rational and human, naive and pertinent. Different social cultures and patterns of behaviour have produced different approaches to this most human of problems and progress is both recent and, for the disabled, painfully slow. Above all it is education, communication and understanding that are needed and this is the common echo of the chapters that follow.

5

Attitudes of society towards sex and the handicapped

MARGARET R. MORGAN

In spite of the rapid development of the 'permissive society' in most countries in the western world, and the much greater freedom in talking about, reading about, looking at and experiencing all aspects of sexual relationships, there is still a great paucity of information about, and a considerable reluctance to face and discuss, the needs and problems of people whose disabilities constitute some form of barrier to the making of normal personal and intimate relationships.

It seems to me, from my reading of reports in the English language, that where this major basic human instinct is mentioned at all, even in recent reports, it is recognized as presenting considerable problems for young handicapped people, but, as the following two extracts indicate, the solutions offered seem to avoid the main issue, that of the recognition of the right to sexuality of the handicapped man or woman. Both reports were published during the past twelve months, the first in Great Britain and the second in the U.S.A.

> Not only do recreational pursuits provide bridges to the world of the non-handicapped; they also provide opportunities to make relations with the opposite sex during

adolescence, when most young people are looking for romance and eventually marriage. This is a particularly neglected aspect of education in living with a handicap, probably because it is so fraught with hurt, damaged self-esteem, and, most important of all, because there are no easy or ready answers. All this, every handicapped young person must face sooner or later; if he can do so with the help of a compassionate, understanding and honest adult, then his (and even more so her) learning will be that much less difficult. Getting to know handicapped people who have made successful marriages may give hope. For some, marriage will be an unlikely goal. The knowledge that some people are successfully and happily wedded to their work or hobby, and through these made firm friendships, may be a consolation if not an aim.
(*Living with Handicap*, 'Report of a working party on children with special needs', National Children's Bureau, 1970).

In the present era of greater freedom in sexual behaviour among non-handicapped groups, it is especially important for professionals to recognise the needs of the multi-handicapped and the difficulty they have in solving their problems within limits acceptable to the community. Where sex education is part of the school curriculum there should be no question of withholding this information from the handicapped student. Where the school system has not accepted this responsibility the private agencies should, in conjunction with parental co-operation, initiate instruction groups. Professionals should create a permissive atmosphere where young persons may feel free to ask questions. Social interaction groups for the multihandicapped should be formed to give them a chance to be with peers of both sexes. The frequent opportunity of non-handicapped young people, in work, study and recreation, to gain confirmation and reinforcement of sexual identity should not be denied to handicapped young people. This workshop made efforts to suggest specific ways to widen the opportunity for some degree of sexual experience for the handicapped that would be comparable to that of their non-handicapped peers. It was necessary, however, to face the fact that despite changing attitudes in the world at large, cultural mores would, at this time, prevent actual translation of these into programme. However, it is essential that professionals be aware of the problem and that they continue, together with young adults who are handicapped, to seek satisfactory answers.

As a beginning, professionals can see that sex education is provided. Knowledge is needed to dispel misinformation, old wives' tales and myths. This should be supplemented with specific knowledge in relation to various disabling conditions.
(*The Second Milestone*, United Cerebral Palsy Associations Inc., New York, 1970).

After reading these two reports I am left with the impression that all we feel able to do is to provide handicapped people with more information, so that they can understand more fully what they are missing! I accept that other reports and more positive papers may well have been published recently in English and other languages, just as I know that in Holland, at least, a joint working party has been set up to look specifically at these problems. I am sure that other countries, too, are working towards facing the situation more honestly and frankly, but what seems interesting is that this is often considered to be predominantly a problem for medical people and, although discussion groups may be arranged for handicapped people, they do not appear to be very adequately represented on the working parties.

I propose to explore the possible reasons for this inability to face the issues squarely, and to do this we need to look at some of the general attitudes towards handicapped people, to see how far these apply to their sexuality and to their personal relationships. To complete the picture, I think we should also look at the attitudes of parents and professional people and then at the attitudes of handicapped people themselves to both the problems and to what others think of them.

This breakdown very conveniently fits in with Erving Goffman's analysis in his book, *Stigma: Notes on the Management of Spoiled Identity*, (Penguin, 1968), and I propose to use his three groupings, the 'Normals', the 'Wise', and the 'Own'. But first, to remind ourselves of Goffman's thesis that minority, different and marginal groups are stigmatized and viewed in different ways by different groups of people.

> The Greeks, who were apparently strong on visual aids, originated the word 'Stigma' to refer to bodily signs designed to expose something unusual and bad about the moral status of the signifier.
>
> The attitudes we normals have towards a person with a Stigma, and the actions we take in regard to him, are well known, since these responses are what benevolent social action is designed to soften and ameliorate. By definition, of course, we believe the person with a stigma is not quite human.

The attitudes of 'Normals', and here I mean the attitudes of the man or woman in the street, or members of the general public, who are not closely connected with handicapped people.

First, most people seem to prefer to think of the handicapped as perpetual 'Peter Pans', who remain appealing and dependent children.

> Only a minority of the population are likely to come into direct contact with cerebral palsy, particularly since so many patients are largely home bound. When they do meet young people suffering from cerebral palsy, it is noticeable that their compassion and desire to help are much more readily stimulated by the appealing child patient than by the adult, who may very often be grotesque in appearance, clumsy in movement and have an uncared-for air.

This attitude also extends to the sexual development of handicapped people and, in my opinion, this is probably the major reason why it is easier to pretend that severely handicapped children will never grow up. People may well have some curiosity about the anatomical and sexual development of physically handicapped people, especially of girls, but it is very difficult for many of the 'normal' general public to face and accept the mature sexuality of people who are physically damaged in one way or another. If one does accept that severely handicapped people grow up and develop sexually, then one is faced with the likelihood that they will have the same drives and needs as everyone else. This leads on to the reality of how these can possibly be satisfied, and satisfied in a way that is seen as ideal?

Second, there is also a tendency on the part of 'normal' people to treat the basic human rights of handicapped people as privileges to be meted out to them, almost as though they were rewards given to children by parents. The corollary of this is a tendency to be shocked when handicapped people act like adults rather than as children, for instance by swearing, drinking and even smoking, let alone caressing and petting each other!

Third, the stigmatization of, and imposition of inferior status on, handicapped people are also very relevant and I should like to examine some of the views on these concepts and to relate them to the sexual field.

A leader in a recent issue of the *Sunday Times* (28 March, 1971) by Jack Ashley, a handicapped Member of Parliament, included these words: 'Severely disabled people are deeply affected by the assumption that they are inferior and should always wait. And it will only be when their incapacity is no longer explicitly, implicitly, deplored that they will have occasion to celebrate a new era.'

Beatrice A. Wright in *Physical Disability, A Psychological Approach* (Harper & Row, 1960) refers to this concept on a number of occasions:

> Some individuals deny the fact that persons with

disabilities are looked down upon. This protest has come not only from those who have a disability but also from professional personnel, such as teachers and rehabilitation workers, actively engaged in disability matters. Perhaps it is felt that to assert the existence of inferiority as an attitude is to affirm it as a fact. Public attitudes are often positive, but negative, deprecating attitudes also exist, although these may be more covert.

Devaluation is expressed in various ways. It is seen in the patronising attitude of the person who gives money to 'help those poor little crippled children'.

The stereotype of a person with a disability typically describes one who has suffered a great misfortune and whose life is consequently disturbed, distorted and damaged for ever.

Inferior status clearly includes inferior sexual development and performance and therefore, more often than not, a denial of the need for fulfilment. There is no doubt that many 'normal' people feel shock and disgust at the thought of severely physically handicapped people having any intimate relationships or sexual intercourse.

In 1972 we should be able to look at and face a little more squarely the reasons for this attitude. New and more explicit manuals on sex techniques appear in the bookshops daily, films for children which leave nothing to the imagination are shown in schools and woman's magazines emphasize the rights of their readers to ensure that they are fully satisfied by their husbands. Knowledge is increasing, techniques no doubt are improving and levels of satisfaction are probably rising, but everyone has an 'ideal' for their sexual relationships, which in reality they may or may not attain. The thought of 'damaged' people indulging in these very intimate relationships, therefore, touches off deeply personal, and probably subconscious, reactions and aversions, and many 'normal' people, being unable to imagine that those whom they see as 'inferior' could possibly achieve the level of satisfaction that they see as ideal, deny their right to or need for any sexual fulfilment at all. It is also probably appropriate to refer here to the castration theory, to which Beatrice Wright (1960) refers:

> Of the many facets of psychoanalysis, however, castration theory is directly related to emotional disturbance occasioned by the sight or thought of disability. A summary of it follows:
>
> In brief, the castration complex comes about as a result of childhood experience. The child soon discovers the meaning of his genital organs and, in his earliest fantasies revolving about the love of the mother, unconsciously 'posits' his penis as a rival to his father's. Fearing revenge from the father, however, the child imagines that retribution will take the form of depriving him of his male organ. Such a drastic procedure would, in his fantasy, be the only appropriate punishment from the father for taboo Oedipal desires in which the mother becomes an incestuous love object. Throughout his childhood, the child may extend these vague fears to encompass the notion that his father will, in one way or another, punish him for his sexual activities in general. Thus his remorse or anxieties about masturbation may be reflecting castratory fears.
>
> The castration complex could, according to psychoanalytic thought, be symbolically brought into play by any remotely analogous equivalent of castration. Thus the loss of a leg, or seeing another person who has lost a leg, may stir up archaic castratory fears. Indeed, the loss of any part of the body, or the sight of such a loss, is said to be symbolically capable of recalling the Oedipal taboo and the father's potential revenge—that of cutting off or mutilating the phallus. Whether or not castration anxiety is universal, and whether or not it necessarily has such ubiquitous effects where it does exist, are matters for conjecture and research. In any case, the clinical evidence is strong that castration anxiety does occur and can ramify to attitudes toward disability.

It does not seem to be extending this theory unjustifiably to use it to explain some of the strong and prejudiced feelings aroused by the thought of any sexual activity on the part of physically handicapped people.

At this point we should probably look at the sexual development and needs of handicapped people. The following quotation from Wright (1960) is relevant:

> There is, however, no systematic evidence to indicate that young persons with disabilities have more troubles in heterosexual adjustments than other young people. Landis and Bolles' study (1942) is the most systematic in this area. It investigated specifically the psychosexual development of women with physical handicaps as compared with physically normal women. The subjects were 17 to 30 years of age. Ratings were made on the basis of controlled interviews. On the characteristics listed below, the group with handicaps differed from the normal groups:

	Percentage of	
	Handicapped	*Physically normal*
First knowledge of sex differences before age 6	11	33
Complete sex information before age 15	11	26
Little or no preparation for menstruation	78	55
No history of masturbation	74	50
Extremely close to family	23	3
No evidence of homoerotic behaviour	23	8
Never been in love	30	3
Never had dates with boys	28	1
First date before age 16	18	52
No evidence of masculine protest	43	26
Recalled a desire to be a boy in childhood	43	69
Attitude of disgust towards sex	7	21

Source: Adapted and abridged from Landis and Bolles (1942).

From these and related data the authors conclude that, in comparison with physically normal women, those with physical handicaps are less autoerotic, are emotionally more dependent on their families, are less homoerotic, have fewer heterosexual contacts, give less evidence of masculine protest, have equal narcissism, and are less emotional about sex in general. Even though the Landis and Bolles women with physical handicaps were slower in dating and falling in love than were their normal controls, they also were less emotional about sex in general and in some ways had fewer knots to untie, such as autoeroticism, homoeroticism, and masculine protest.

We have to accept, not only from the results of surveys but from our own experience of cerebrally palsied young people, that development may be, and often is, delayed, and that full social maturity and competence will not be possible for those who are significantly intellectually damaged. It seems evident, however, that maturation can be helped or hindered, brought to full adult status or cut off at an adolescent or pre-adolescent stage by the attitudes and actions of other people, and here those most closely involved with the handicapped have the greatest part to play. So we turn now to:

The attitudes of the 'Wise' To quote Goffman (1963), 'to borrow a term once used by homosexuals—the "wise", namely, persons who are normal but whose special situation has made them intimately privy to the secret life of the stigmatized individual and sympathetic with it, and who find themselves accorded a measure of acceptance, a measure of courtesy membership in the clan.'

This group includes professional people working closely with the handicapped and also their families and close relatives. To take the professionals first. People working closely with physically handicapped adolescents and adults are clearly aware of the facts of physiological development and sexual maturity, but there often seems to be a denial of the handicapped person's sexuality and psycho-sexual needs.

Some staff working in residential centres will say that many cerebrally palsied people have diminished sexual drives or are undersexed and that it is best not to force discussions or the passing on of factual information to handicapped people, as this may only raise feelings, emotions and problems that would otherwise have lain dormant. These may be valid arguments. The sexual drives and demands of severely physically handicapped people may be less intense than those of unhandicapped men and women, and it may be sensible to withold information and stimulation if people are not going to be able to satisfy their needs or reach sexual fulfilment. But is this a denial of the right of an individual to become sexually mature as a man or woman? Obviously, the level of intellectual understanding and potential for social maturity are relevant and for some the full range of adult personal relationships will not be possible. Are we, however, sometimes tempted to impute immaturity or retardation to someone who could reach adult sexual status because it is easier to evade than to deal with the problems that might arise? In the case of severely handicapped men and women other people often have to make moral decisions for them and they are, therefore, in a position to facilitate or stifle growth and development. It seems important to ensure that we only continue to make decisions on behalf of those who are never likely to be mature enough to choose or decide for themselves and that we guard against conspiring to go on making decisions for those who could be helped to make more mature moral choices for themselves.

In recent years there has been increasing emphasis on the opposite extreme of attitudes, that handicapped people are entitled, by right, to have anything that they want or need. How far does this extend to meeting the sexual needs of handicapped people? Where severely handicapped men and women are concerned, what services should staff or friends be prepared, or expected, to offer? Are there any circumstances in which a member of staff or friend should help a handicapped person to masturbate or to achieve sexual intercourse, either with another handicapped person or by offering their own services? These are thorny questions, but ones that face wardens and staff in residential settings and they have to be resolved in as humane and understanding a way as possible.

It seems that a course halfway between the two extremes will most adequately meet the combined needs of the individual, the community and the staff. Sexual needs must be recognized and, wherever possible, handicapped men and women should be enabled to develop to their maximum sexual maturity. At the same time, it is essential to recognize and to help individual handicapped people to recognize and cope with the fact that they may be denied the full expression of their manhood and womanhood. I have what may well be unjustifiable confidence that, when faced with reality and the possibility of making moral decisions for themselves, many handicapped people can be helped to live with the situation.

And now, to turn to the attitudes of parents towards the sexuality of their handicapped son or daughter. Clearly this is an area of anxiety and mixed emotions and feelings for most parents, who must look forward to the puberty and adolescence of a severely handicapped boy or girl with some apprehension. How will they, for instance, as parents, and how will the young handicapped person, individually and together, cope with the practical problems? This is of particular concern where heavily handicapped or retarded girls and their menstrual problems are concerned, but it also involves the sexual development of handicapped boys. What will happen about their wet dreams and what about shaving? On a very practical level many a father must wonder if he is going to have to continue to shave his badly handicapped son day after day. These problems seem fairly straightforward to those of us who are so used to coping with them, but each set of parents anticipates and has to face all these issues anew as their own son or daughter approaches the adolescent stage. And mixed with the worry is probably some pleasure and satisfaction when the handicapped girl has her first menstrual period and the boy has an emission. This, at least, proves they are normal in one area of their development. Other conflicting emotions are aroused too, those of sadness and regret at what the boy or girl is probably going to miss in adult life—marriage, companionship, a home of one's own and children.

Physical maturity brings with it the possibility of an unwanted pregnancy for the less physically handicapped, but perhaps very inexperienced and socially retarded girl. Clearly, whoever is responsible for the girl has a duty to ensure that she understands as much as she is capable of absorbing and that guidance and supervision are available, but from the very limited experience that we have, we have found that some mothers have not been as outraged as we had imagined they would be when their daughters became pregnant and, on the contrary, a few have clearly seen this as a reinforcement of their daughter's attractiveness and normality.

Wright (1960) emphasizes the problems of the marginal position of handicapped young persons between adulthood and childhood.

> In our society, the status of full adulthood is generally withheld until the advent of two outstanding circumstances: economic independence and marriage . . . Where circumstances prolong the period of economic dependence, postpone marriage, or disallow sufficient emotional separation from the parent, then the position of the individual as an adult, no matter what his age, is apt to be tenuous and, like that of the adolescent, marginal between adulthood and childhood. He may well continue to experience conflicts with parental authority resulting from such marginality, to feel devaluated as an incomplete adult, and to show inconsistent, exaggerated, and emotional behaviour typical of conflicting overlapping situation. It may very well be that the fact of disability in many cases tends to prolong the adolescent period.

Parents can however, be helped to recognize these problems and tensions and some will then be able to help the handicapped boy or girl to rebel and find ways of reinforcing his or her own identity as an emerging adult, a separate person from his or her parents. This is, however, extremely difficult for, necessarily, very dependent young men or women and sometimes a time spent away from home with a peer group will help to establish their adult roles, including their self image of their sexual status. This now leads on to the last group:

The attitudes of their 'Own' That is, how handicapped people see their own sexual roles and others' attitudes towards them. Here I would like to quote from another book entitled *Stigma: the experience of disability* (ed., Paul Hunt, Geoffrey Chapman, 1966), which is a collection of essays written by handicapped men and women. These two quotations are from an essay by a severely handicapped man entitled 'The Chatterley Syndrome', which uses the crippled condition and impotency of Sir Clifford Chatterley, Lady Chatterley's husband, to illustrate the situation of the handicapped person.

> 'What a piece of work is man!' marvelled Hamlet, though perhaps he was being ironic. However one rates the human species, a man must be considered as a whole. His body is an incredibly wonderful piece of fully automated engineering, but in itself it is not a man. His mind, soul, spirit is an even more wonderful and complex thing, but in itself it still does not constitute a man. To make a man you must put the two together. He is more than the mere sum of these parts, but a deficiency in one means a deficiency in the whole. Lawrence's view that after Sir Clifford became a cripple he was no longer a man is extreme, but it contains more truth than we may like to admit. A cripple is still a man, but, as it were, on a smaller scale. His totality is diminished, his image distorted. He is not a whole.
>
> It inevitably follows, then, that there must always be

this barrier of difference and distortion between us and the inhabitants of the normal world. No matter how close our individual relationships with our able-bodied friends may seem, it is impossible for them to have the same kinds of relationship with us that they can have with others from their own world. This is perhaps the most bitter truth of all, the one that most of us find the hardest to accept—that we are forever barred from the deepest and most intimate levels of human intercourse. I can already hear the shocked cries of denial: 'He never thinks of me as being a cripple!' Not consciously, perhaps, but in his innermost heart he knows you are, and he always will. It is this fundamental unconscious knowledge, rather than sexual frustration or the sheer struggle of looking after a badly crippled partner, that breaks up so many marriages between the inhabitants of these two worlds. There are barriers that even love cannot penetrate—always assuming there can be complete love between a complete person and an incomplete one, which I doubt. (In parenthesis, it might be objected that this gloomy theory appears to break down when one considers the blind. According to my argument, the blind, lacking one of the most important and valuable of faculties, are as incomplete as the crippled, and, like them, must be separated from the normal world; yet marriages between the blind and the sighted seem on the whole to be as happy and permanent as those between two sighted people. The answer would seem to be that a great many blind people never leave the normal world, which continues to accept them to a much greater extent than it accepts us. For some obscure Jungian reason, blindness hasn't the same sinister associations that physical abnormality has in the collective unconscious: indeed, it has strong associations with poetry and wisdom—blind poets and sages abound in history and legend.)

The least abstract and theoretical incentive the adolescent cripple possesses is the sexual one: his glands have undergone the normal disturbances, he suffers the normal

> torments and dreams the normal dreams. Unless he is particularly unattractive, he probably won't have much difficulty in acquiring a girlfriend, her feelings towards him largely genuine enough but inevitably containing a certain amount of pity and curiosity. He may be deeply in love and think he has detected signs of a similar feeling in her, and the relationship may reach quite a high level of mutual affection as the girl's original curiosity is satisfied and she learns to appreciate him for his qualities as an individual; but pity will rarely be entirely eliminated. Eventually a climax will be reached, a crisis, after which the affair will either plane down to a lower, more realistic level, or—and this is much more likely—stop abruptly. He will console himself by thinking that this kind of thing happens to everybody, crippled or not, and that there are other fish in the sea. But although one or two more may swim into his net, the odds are overwhelming that they will swim out again, and bitterly he will begin to realize that he is in for the lonely, perverted life of the enforced celibate.

And from another essay, this time by a handicapped woman.

> In his encounter with society the invalid rarely meets active dislike or disgust. But if he ventures into the world of love, such feelings are not so far off. It happens, on occasion, that a disabled person falls in love with a normal member of society. Sometimes it even happens that this love is reciprocated. It is interesting to observe the different reactions to such—one is tempted to say—a social outrage. One gets the impression that the invalid has more or less committed an indecent act. He isn't supposed to have such feelings. And the 'normal' partner in such a crazy adventure—well, he is hardly considered normal at all. He ought to have his head examined. Some people seem to feel offended at the thought that a 'disabled' person feels the same way as a 'normal' person does. This reaction is not apparent when invalids marry one another. As long as they keep to themselves society

> doesn't really mind. The invalid may marry another of his kind, and live happily or unhappily ever after. Society doesn't greatly care whether he is happy or unhappy as long as society isn't troubled. A wall is raised between the 'normal' world and the world of the disabled—a wall invisible and hard and cold as unbreakable glass.

Wright (1960) emphasizes the importance of physique in adolescence and in establishing one's sexual role and identity and this is obviously very relevant where physically handicapped young people and their self-image are concerned.

> The young person looks at his physique in the new light of sex appropriateness. Not only do the more purely biological urges contribute to this awareness, but the values of society also bring tremendous pressure on the young person to examine himself in terms of the criteria of his sex role. Particularly during adolescence, these criteria follow rigid standards as to what the feminine and masculine model should be. Marriage and children are deeply ingrained values of society and, in fact, are often necessary passports to full adult status. Small wonder, then, that the adolescent as he grows into adulthood keeps testing himself as to whether he can make the grade. His final score requires not one look at the self but many as each experience with members of the opposite sex is assessed. The status value of physique assumes tremendous potency because of its identification with rigid and idealized notions of what is admissible to each sex. For him [the handicapped young person], physique becomes evaluated in terms of rigid standards of sex appropriateness and, like other adolescents, he has an intense interest in all matters that have to do with the establishment of his status as a man or woman.

The comment of a young spastic woman made to me some years ago has, I am sure, been repeated by many others at many different times. 'The fact that we have a handicap doesn't mean that we don't have the same emotions and desires as everyone else, though people seem very shocked when we do.' I would like to refer briefly to the attitude of handicapped people to sexual relationships and marriage as expressed at a conference of over 250 handicapped people, most of whom were cerebrally palsied, held in the University of Reading, England, in 1969, under the auspices of the Association of '62 Clubs and the Spastics Society. I had the privilege of presenting a paper on 'Marriage and the Handicapped' (in *Third International '62 Club Conference Papers*, ed. William Hargreaves, Spastics Society, 1969) and in it I raised a number of controversial questions, to be discussed and answered when the conference broke up into small discussion groups. The reports of these groups make interesting reading and they remind us forcibly that handicapped people are well able to look at problems affecting themselves and form conclusions, if only they are allowed and enabled to do so.

On the whole, the conclusions strongly supported high moral standards for handicapped people, standards that were probably more applicable a couple of generations ago than today, but this, perhaps, reflects the dependence of some handicapped people on the views and standards of the adult figures from their childhood days.

The following is an extract from the report of one of the discussion groups:

> The first question was trial marriage, and most of us have come to the conclusion that as trial marriage is not acceptable to society generally, why should it be accepted by us? Of course, we have more problems to overcome and somebody said—wouldn't it be better to have a trial marriage to see how you got on, and if you got on at all? But we thought this was not a good idea, for most of us women, at least, it is terribly important for us to feel secure, and it could produce very insecure feelings if you are in a trial marriage and your partner suddenly gets fed up with you and he can hop it. It is terribly important for

physically handicapped people to feel settled and sure, so for us trial marriage is not acceptable at all.

The next question was about companionate marriages. On the whole it was felt that this was a good thing, if a couple obviously were very fond of each other and enjoyed each other's company, and were aware of the fact that it was not going to be a full marriage but wanted to spend the rest of their lives together. Here, a legal ceremony binding them together could be very helpful. We were thinking mainly of people in residential homes or centres and if they accept that they will not be able to consummate the marriage the legal relation can give them a secure feeling. One comment was 'Why get married at all?' Well, as I said before, the ceremony is binding and it does make you secure, to know that somebody is going to look after you when you are old. There are problems, of course, but on the whole it was considered to be a good thing for people for whom the full marriage relationship was not possible.

The third question was about marriage between two heavily handicapped people, and when I first saw this question I thought it was like the one before, then I was told very firmly that I was to read the question again; and that the emphasis was on the personal and intimate help that might be required.

All through their lives heavily handicapped people have had to have help, personal help, and we come to accept it, but it is quite a different thing to accept the intimate help that you may have to have to make a full marriage, and it is all very well for people like myself who are slightly handicapped to sit judgment and say 'I couldn't bear the thought of a third person coming between myself and my husband,' and we wondered what heavily handicapped people would feel about this.

We had one in our group and he was very brave and told us that he would not accept this kind of help at all, and it was just a thing that they would have to come to terms with—if they could not have intercourse on their

> own, then they would not have a full marriage, and it was something that they would have to learn to accept.
>
> The last question concerned free sexual relationships without marriage. Most of the group were against this, and nowadays you see so much about the permissive society and how sex is much more free, but I am sure that if a survey was done throughout the country the people who do not agree with this would probably be in the majority. The group, on the whole, did not agree with sexual relationships without marriage, even for handicapped people.
> (*op. cit.*)

And from a recently published survey of handicapped people in the London area:

> Most younger single persons felt that their attitudes towards marriage remained unchanged by disability; indeed, some were planning to get married in the near future. But attitudes towards marriage appeared to be affected by degree of incapacity. In general, those who were severely or very severely incapacitated felt that they were unlikely to get married. They tended to rationalize their disappointment by distinguishing the care required of a spouse from the outset of marriage from that necessitated by the onset of disability in the course of marriage: the latter, but not the former, was considered to be acceptable. Altogether, two-thirds of younger single persons felt that they would get married.
> (*Registered as Disabled*, Sally Sainsbury, Bell, 1970).

I would like to conclude with a few personal views about the current situation. First, much though we may deplore some aspects of the permissive society, there are ways in which it can be of positive assistance to the handicapped. The greater freedom and frankness of expression, the growing tolerance of some forms of deviation and the acknowledgement that perversions exist should help people to react less violently and emotionally to sexual relationships between people who are physically damaged in one way or another. On the other hand, what may be freedom of expression and action amongst young people and the 'intelligentsia' still seems to have strongly pornographic and 'voyeuristic' elements as far as a large proportion of the general public is concerned and this may not encourage healthy and positive attitudes towards the sexuality of handicapped people.

Second, my view is that young handicapped people with a reasonable level of understanding have a right to be allowed, in fact to be helped, to develop as fully mature men and women and to make moral choices and decisions for themselves. After all, you can decide to remain celibate or learn to live a celibate life and to cope with the physical and emotional tensions and pressures in one way or another. It is human nature to press for something that others are denying to you or depriving you of, and you can be much more rational about decision-making if some element of choice is available to you.

Third, the areas for action seem to be:

(1) to make more adequate provision for basic sex education and also a broader based general education, including courses on human development, interpersonal and group relationships, ethics and philosophy. Much more adequate and realistic counselling for those planning to get married is also required.
(2) To provide more opportunities for peer group discussions, both between individuals and in groups.
(3) To encourage the normal adolescent progression from homosexual to heterosexual relationships within the peer group.
(4) To consider our roles as 'helping' people. Practical, material and economic supports and help can make marriage, or sexual relationships outside marriage, possible for even severely physically handicapped people. But who makes the crucial and final decisions?

We [i.e. handicapped people] can witness to the truth that a person's dignity does not rest even in his consciousness, and certainly that it does not rest in his beauty, age, intelligence or colour. Those of us with unimpaired minds but severely disabled bodies, have a unique opportunity to show other people not only that our big difference from them does not lessen our worth, but also that no difference between men, however real, unpleasant and disturbing, does away with their right to be treated as fully human.

We face more obviously than most the universal problem of coming to terms with the fact of man's individuality and loneliness. If we begin to accept our own special peculiarity, we shall be in a position to help others accept even their own difference from everyone else. These two acceptances are bound up together. People's shocked reactions to the obvious deviant often reflect their own deepest fears and difficulties, their failure to accept themselves as they really are, and the other person simply as 'other'.

The disabled person's 'strangeness' can manifest and symbolize all differences between human beings. In his relations with more nearly normal people he may become a medium for reconciling them to the fact of these differences, and demonstrate their relative unimportance compared to what we have in common.

6

Marriage and the handicapped

A. H. SUTTON

'You know we're frauds!' My wife had turned to me in bed with this frank and surprising statement. It sounded an interesting discussion point so I determined to pursue it. She was in fact referring to my involvement with the subject of marriage and the handicapped. 'Perhaps you should have been married six times and have had a working knowledge of several handicaps to be competent to discuss such a subject,' she suggested. In point of fact I have been married only once so far and can claim a personal knowledge only of cerebral palsy, but I was not swayed by my wife's argument, for the fact that we are both quite seriously handicapped, married and leading a comparatively normal and independent life does provide a useful and credible basis for such a discussion.

Before I refer to my marriage, I should perhaps comment on my handicap. I had the privilege recently of appearing in a film made by the Spastics Society in London which was an attempt to highlight the problems of the cerebral palsied adult entering society. I thought that I made a great many dubious statements in this film, but one struck me as having more than a ring of truth. I said that if it were possible to take away my twisted limbs, peel off my peculiar facial expressions, and remove all traces of my athetoid condition, you would be left with a normal man. Trite perhaps, but I remain convinced that in the context of the film which was intended for the general public this was a valid statement and one which must have had impact. For as long as I can remember I have been conscious of two 'me's—the outer casing which is visible to the world and the inner substance which is not. The outer casing is, of course, my body, and is the façade by which, in all but a few circumstances, the world judges me. The inner part is my mind, my character, my conscience, and my true being. So it is, of course, with everybody, but this concept will help what follows to seem more meaningful. The fact is that my life has been a constant conflict involving these two parts.

The world judges you by your appearance—indeed it judges almost everything by appearances. When interviewed some time ago on radio, and asked to comment on his success as an entertainer, that remarkable man Sammy Davis junior said that he did not feel that he had done too badly for himself despite his handicaps. The interviewer was audibly shocked, and pursued the matter, enquiring what these handicaps were. With his customary timing Sammy Davis replied, 'I'm a one-eyed Jewish Negro.' The interviewer passed it off as a joke, but I did not take it to be one, nor can I persuade myself that Sammy Davis intended it as such. He was, I'm sure, aware of the humour of the situation, but that's a vastly different thing.

As a child I don't remember much about my life, but what I do remember seems significant. I adored riding my tricycle. I used to spend hours on it when the weather was fine—it was about the only thing I could do. I didn't enjoy it when I fell off, and this I did regularly about twice a week. I just lay there and waited for news to get back to my mother who would come and pick me up and mend me. But even at this time I was conscious of my body, and of my appearance. Kids used to come up and ask me what my name was, didn't I know it? What time was it? Why couldn't I talk properly (they couldn't understand the answers I gave them), why was I shaking? etc. It didn't take long for me to appreciate the situation, yet I knew the answers to their questions.

Later in life, in my early teens, this problem of appearance became worse. I became very self-conscious, and this in turn made my speech, already poor, worse still. My father, a successful businessman, had friends to whom he introduced me, but I could never say anything which they could interpret, and I could see their growing embarrassment, sometimes writing me off as imbecilic. I had at these times to retain a very firm grasp of my inner being to avoid . . . to avoid what? I don't know . . . possibly insanity. I remember on one occasion my father, to his credit, resolutely introduced me to a business colleague who knew a bit about cerebral palsy, just enough to know that I wasn't silly, and this chap owned a particularly fast car. I had for many years possessed a very keen interest in cars and knew practically all that one could know about this particular car. I think the interest I had in the car must have alleviated my self-consciousness, for I suddenly asked him the most searching technical question about his car, in clear speech which he understood. He was surprised, my father was a little surprised, but I wasn't. My mind, my inner being, had triumphed over its outer casing, and that man respected me for my question. He overlooked the outer casing and penetrated into the inner 'me'. Incidentally, he didn't know the answer to my question about the car, which had cost him about £6,000, and I remember thinking how ridiculous *he* was to own this type of car yet not to know much about its specification!

Age increased my immobility and problems became worse. My family were kind, but I was completely dependent upon them for my contacts with society. One's teenage years are normally one's worst, and with me it was no exception. I think the complete realization of my hopeless situation, or so it seemed, came when I saw boys of my own age walking out with girls. Sex had suddenly assumed an importance and a new significance. The first sexual urges I experienced brought with them probably the culmination of the conflict I mentioned earlier—the conflict which sprang out of knowledge that mentally I was alert, but physically repulsive. I sat in my room alone and despaired. No one will doubt that even the heaviest handicap is necessarily a bar to sexual arousal. Who can forecast sexual attraction? It is something one can seek, for example, at the cinema, at a bunny club, at a house of pleasure, or it can occur unexpectedly in a bus queue, at the office, in a home for the cerebral palsied. It does not necessarily depend upon nudity, or upon voluntary acts. The fall of a girl's hair, the tone of her voice as she speaks, the cut of a man's jaw, the width of his shoulders—each of these is sufficient in itself to achieve sexual arousal in the most severely handicapped person. It has been my experience that sex drives are just as prevalent with the handicapped, and sexual appetites demand some gratification. At this crucial period in my life my parents were very naturally concerned about my future. I am what might be termed a 'first generation' spastic. By this I mean that I was born just late enough to benefit from early specialized treatment. I attended two special schools for the cerebral palsied where much was done to improve a very severe athetoid condition. However, it became clear when I was about twelve or thirteen years of age that the extent to which I could improve physically would be limited, and a decision was made to concentrate on my education. To give some idea of the severity of my condition I ought perhaps to explain that I could not feed myself at all at the age of twelve, and I could not use a self-propelling wheelchair until I was seventeen. At fifteen the local education authority which was paying for my schooling refused to pay out any more money, and I would perhaps have sat at home, rotting like a vegetable had my father not had the foresight, and the means, to allow me to further my education. He realised that if I was to achieve anything in this world it would be as a result of education. I studied at home, and at evening institutes, for six years, until I had attained the necessary academic qualifications required for university entrance.

I had studied hard. I think that in study I found an outlet, a release from the problems of living in a world where I was something of an alien, a social reject. I was feeding my inner being, and ignoring my outer casing. At least, for the majority of the time. . . . There were occasions on which the conflict recurred—I can remember experiencing acute embarrassment when I first attended evening classes. But I quickly settled this by achieving better marks than any of my fellow class-mates. I was guided in my home study by a private tutor who was himself disabled. The friendship and encouragement I received from this man I look back on as being of paramount importance to me, and I think it must have been a period of challenge for him too. He is now the Head of a further education centre for the cerebral palsied in England.

With this academic success and the greater awareness of life which accompanied it came greater self-confidence. I was learning to live with my handicap. There was a greater purpose to my life, albeit an academic purpose, and what people thought of my appearance mattered less. About this time I met a truly gifted physio-therapist who offered to give me treatment at home. The results were slow but positive. Apart from this man's special ability, I am unable to account for what was a dramatic improvement in my physical condition. At the age of twenty-one I had passed the physical examination necessary for the issue by the state of an invalid car!

My horizons immediately widened. Although confined to a wheelchair, I was able to lead an independent life for the first time. The joy of being able to go to the cinema, provided there were no steps, or the theatre without depending upon one's relatives was indescribable. Horizons wider than I had ever dared to hope for opened up before me, and a most cherished hope, that of a place at university, became a reality. At university, I thought, I would integrate socially with people of my own age for the first time, people who would be able to overlook the outer casing and have the intellect to accept me for myself.

It seems ludicrous that I could have been so naive as to have believed that this could have happened—of course, it didn't! At least, not generally. I did make a few close friends at university, people who were very kind to me, but not necessarily the people whom I would have chosen for friends. There were a couple of do-gooders, and a chap who came from Trinidad and who was faced with much the same integration problem as mine. As for girls, well, I think it took me about three weeks to find out what they thought of me. I remember I had bought a couple of tickets for a jazz concert (I wrote the jazz column for the university paper at this time) and although it took some doing I did screw up the necessary courage to ask a particular girl to go with me—or rather meet me there so that she would not be troubled about getting into the building with my wheelchair. She smiled and declined with thanks, saying she didn't care for jazz. This was my first attempt at dating a girl, and there was a certain glory in doing it, so it didn't worry me too much that she declined. I said fine, but she didn't know what she was missing, making quite sure that she understood I was referring to the music, of course, and assuring her that I quite understood. What did throw me a little was to see her that very night sitting three rows away with another young man. I told her next day that I was pleased that she had taken my advice and decided to sample the delights of the Modern Jazz Quartet—it revealed an open mind. I don't believe we spoke again for the remainder of our four-year course . . . but I learned a lot.

Academically, university was exciting; socially, it was a drag. On reflection, I think this was very substantially my own fault. I can still hear ringing in my ears my course tutor's advice: 'Don't be so bloody independent—people are ready to help, let them!' Yes, I was absolutely determined that I was going to get through university without being carried on other people's backs.

So far I have discussed almost exclusively myself and my handicap, and very little about marriage. It is necessary to understand the circumstances under which I met the girl who was to become my wife, to appreciate what issues were uppermost in my mind when I first saw Joan.

I had been spending much of my spare time at a club for

disabled drivers and finding people there who accepted me readily, and extended real, warm friendship to me. One day I went along to a club meeting and there was Joan. I was immediately attracted to her, and she chatted to me in a way that revealed total acceptance. I saw her more and more frequently, and we spent more and more time together. At first I was reluctant to admit even to myself that this was anything more than just friendship, but there came a time when I went to Spain and Portugal for three months as part of my university studies. One can do a lot of thinking in three months—a lot of self-analysis. What was I doing? Was I being fair to myself, was I risking ruining two lives? Had I a future? Would I ever become financially independent? Would all my years of study culminate in my being able to support myself, let alone a wife? Of one thing I was sure—Joan was the right person, and she was aware of what she was letting herself in for. She was, after all, a mature young woman, with an intimate knowledge of the problems of a handicap. No doubt about it, she was a damm sight more mature than I, having overcome a very crippling disease and having earned her own living in the outside world for a number of years. If she was prepared to take the risk, should I deny myself the opportunity of the happiness which I confidently foresaw? Clearly not! It was a calculated risk which we both accepted.

You will see from what I have just said that Joan's handicap made her more attractive to me. I felt that we had a better chance of a happy and successful life together because she was handicapped. After five years of marriage I still feel the same, and I think that it is significant that although we have undergone the occasional period of marital strain, neither of us has ever complained about the other's handicap. I have often idly wondered whether had I married a non-disabled girl she would have put up with my odd ways, and the restrictions imposed by my handicap. Of course, there can be no answer to this question, and this matter is one which only the two persons concerned can decide. The decision must be theirs, and theirs alone. I do recall in Dr Carlson's book *Born That Way* a stern warning that it was easy for the cerebral palsied to choose entirely the wrong partner simply out of gratitude. Christie Brown in *My Left Foot* warmed to a smile from a beautiful air hostess, only to discover it was motivated by pity. Gratitude and pity are not nouns which Joan and I recognize within the concept of our marriage.

So, together we decided on marriage, but I was not prepared to get engaged officially until I had a job. I felt it important that I had at least the promise of future security to offer her. My graduation from university and our engagement were celebrated on the same day. My future wife's parents were pleased, if apprehensive, whilst mine tolerated the situation. My mother feared for us, and in her own heart I'm sure she believed that I had doubled my problems, not halved them. My father opposed the marriage, and continued to do so until about a fortnight before the wedding—not because he disapproved of Joan, no one who has the least knowledge of her could do that—but because he, too, foresaw a bleak future for us. I think it had caught them both off-balance and they were unable to react rationally. I had not really very much idea of my own future. I saw the immediate tasks in hand to be, first, to make a success of my job (which entailed living and working ninety miles away from home), and second, to convince everyone that we were going to manage well together. I achieved both of these objectives. In fact, I made the second point so hard to friends in the new city in which I was working that they began to suspect that it was to be a marriage of convenience. The truth was that I was unwilling still to admit that this was love. Love implies passionate impulse, romanticism, poetry, and flowers. We were concerned more with hard economics—the problem of finding convenient accommodation, worrying whether we could manage, after all . . .

A lawyer friend of mine, himself spastic, suggested a trial marriage. This I rejected instantly, not as might be supposed because of visions of an irate mother-in-law, or quasi-mother-in-law pursuing me with a hatchet, not because of religious qualms, but because I knew that if we once had one day together as man and wife we would not be willing to give up the ideal and admit defeat.

For similar reasons, we both agreed to practise contraception when we married. It was essential that our marriage should not have to withstand the extra strain of having a baby. The wisdom of this has since been proved by friends of ours who have not taken the same precautions and have imposed almost intolerable strains upon their marriage. The importance of contraception in a handicapped marriage cannot be overstressed, I feel. I personally have little time for those who say that a child is essential to a marriage—free contraception should be available to all who seek it. No one should have an unwanted child.

So we found a bungalow and got married. Joan was cool, calm and collected. My athetosis was tolerable, although I had a frightful cold. The severest strain was probably on our parents: my father-in-law suffered a coronary attack only days afterwards. After a short honeymoon we settled down to our new life together. Now the strain was on Joan for whom this was a completely new role: that of a housewife. It was a tremendous upheaval for her, and I willingly forgave the floods of tears she shed quite frequently during the first few weeks of married life. In all, life proved easier than we had imagined. We settled into our new environment quite well. Neighbours gave us strange looks for a while, and I was asked one or twice how my sister was, and hawkers would ask if my father was at home, but when it was seen that really we lived quite ordinary lives we were accepted. We were even honoured enough one night to be asked to look after a neighbour's daughter who had taken quite a fancy to us although she was only about five years old.

What are my views now, looking back on five years of married life? Primarily, I think, surprise at how little is done to encourage the handicapped to live as normal lives as they possibly can. For a country proud of its social services I can only say that, with a few notable exceptions, the United Kingdom is a disgrace. We still have, I believe, cerebral palsied people living in geriatric wards in hospitals, the Spastics Society is still finding cerebral palsied people who never received treatment in their lives. This is inevitable, of course, but when will the government wake up to the fact that it costs less to set up persons in private flats, to encourage them to live normal lives, to earn their own living, than it does to keep them for the duration of their lives in institutions? Life is expensive and difficult for the handicapped person, and I firmly believe that there should be greater incentive for him to earn his own living. What incentive do Joan and I receive? We get a modest grant towards the maintenance of our motor-car. We elect to receive this grant, instead of two invalid cars which are so unreliable that they constitute a greater handicap in themselves, and a reduction in the rateable value on the bungalow in which we live. We also receive free road tax for our motor-car, and I am issued with free wheelchairs. This is the sum total of the benefits we receive from the state. The new Chronically Sick and Disabled Persons Act is a step in the right direction but even this seems in danger of misinterpretation by local authorities. If lack of money is the drawback, as it always seems to be, then I suggest, a critical look should be taken at that redundant and highly questionable charity payment in a country already overpopulated, the family allowance.

Second, I think there should be a far greater attempt made by the Spastics Society to educate the parents of cerebral palsied children. I attribute much of the happiness and success of my own marriage to the fact that my job took us away from an environment where the natural tendency was to love and to shield the child from the knocks of the cruel world. It grieves me to say this, because I have the deepest love and respect for my parents, but their attitude was almost responsible for ruining my life. And they did it out of kindness.

Next, being myself concerned with education and training, I would like to put forward a powerful plea for a more analytical approach towards the training of higher-intellect spastic people. The education and training of such people should be controlled and channelled towards certain professions in which people with similar handicaps, or similar degrees of handicap, are known to function capably. Ideally, no spastic should be allowed to flounder for a profession or occupation as I did.

Last, whilst readily acknowledging that there is and will always be a role for the special school, may I say that I am convinced that it should be the aim of everyone concerned with the cerebral palsied child's education to integrate him with able-bodied children at the earliest possible moment. No matter how good the education is at a special school, the child will lose by not mixing with other children, and this will almost inevitably give rise to the attitudes which so dogged my early years.

If the four points were to be fully implemented, as ultimately they must be, there is no reason why persons with handicaps even greater than Joan's and mine should not lead happy and full lives within the state of matrimony. My wife goes about her daily chores, I earn the living; we have friends who accept us; our bungalow is indistinguishable from the neighbouring bungalows except that possibly ours is a little better kept. My wife helps me to dress; I help her to bath; we have sexual intercourse frequently; we row about my driving; she never has enough housekeeping money; she always lacks something to wear for that special occasion: in fact, it's all very normal. Perhaps my wife was right after all. Maybe we are frauds.

7

The problems of sex and handicap in Sweden: an investigation

M.-B. BERGSTROM-WALAN

This investigation was undertaken on behalf of the Swedish organization, SVCR (The Swedish Central Committee for Rehabilitation), and the purpose of the research was to study the knowledge and attitudes towards sex among the physically handicapped young people staying in and/or going to special schools for the physically handicapped. The boys and girls who were involved in the research came from three different institutions for physically handicapped in Sweden. The year of the investigation was 1969–70 and includes boys and girls from sixteen to twenty-five years of age—forty boys and thirty-five girls—seventy-five altogether. The investigation was made with the help of a standard questionnaire and was in the main the same instrument that has been used for the Royal State Investigation for Young People in Sweden's ordinary school system. However, in this investigation, more emphasis was placed on expected attitudes towards sex and sexual behaviour among the people working in the institutions, in view of the importance of good relationships between the pupils and their teachers, more especially since they spend so much time together.

The following fields were investigated:

Sex education, its contents and extent and audiovisual aids.

The knowledge among the pupils about sexual and personal relationships.

Attitudes towards sex and sex education, and the need for such education.

The pupils' information sources on sexual and personal relationships from outside school.

Norms for sexual relationships between young people of the same age.

The pupils' estimation of the staff's opinion on sex and sexual behaviour.

The pupils' estimation of their own future in sex relationships and the obstacles facing them in this area.

Anonymity was maintained throughout the whole investigation.

The technical system for the statistical method was the Manual Registration Method (KH system), in which every separate variable has its own separate registration card.

Discussion

One of the goals of the investigation was to estimate the possibility of:

(1) Correcting mistakes in sexual education.
(2) Trying to match the education provided to the needs of the pupils.
(3) Using the technical-pedagogical opportunities that the school has today and to make new aids.
(4) Employing discussions to break down anxiety about sexual life.
(5) Correcting negative attitudes towards people's deviate sexual behaviour.
(6) Eliminating or lessening the difficulties pupils seem to have in their contact with both their class-mates and the adults in their lives.

During personal conversations relating to the question of sexuality, the need was often expressed for the inclusion of individual sexual counselling for those who want it. There are many reasons that make this difficult, especially the lack of trained personnel. It is difficult to find teachers in sex education, and even more difficult to find separate counsellors and advisers. The pupils clearly prefer that the person who gives this advice should not be a member of the regular staff. But what kind of professional person should then be employed? There is a need for experiment at some educational establishments for the physically handicapped, and from those findings a code of practice could be built up.

Result and some conclusions

More than 40 per cent of the pupils involved stated that they had received sex education, and 37 per cent stated that this education included questions with respect to sexual life, while only 19 per cent stated that the education also included 'The Relativity of the Norms'. About 43 per cent stated that they had received education about contraception. Boys and girls had, with few exceptions, been educated together and had also had the opportunity to discuss the subject. On the whole, the pupils had regarded the manner in which this had been done as being positive.

With regard to the questions about sex knowledge, the technical questions were answered well, but the answers about hormones and conception were much more vague. In spite of the positive attitudes towards sex education, the pupils stated, however, that they would like more sex education and more opportunities for discussion. They wanted more films, film-strips and more literature on the subject. The possibility of having personal conversations about sexual questions, including their own sexual problems, was requested by about 60 per cent, and, of these, 70 per cent would not talk to anyone belonging to the staff of the institution. Probably they felt a lack of communication with, and an understanding of, their problems on the part of the staff. In this investigation, 80 per cent of the pupils live in residential institutions and, of these 73 per cent shared rooms. According to the rules at one of these institutions, the pupils were allowed to visit each others rooms, and at this particular institution efforts were being made to introduce mixed sections at the boarding-school.

In answer to the question about who should provide sex education in school, 52 per cent felt that this person should be a visiting expert and not one of the regular teachers. Regarding attitudes towards sexual relationships between young people in the same age-group, 40 per cent felt that it was sufficient to have a relationship with a person seen only occasionally, while 47 per cent felt that a continuing relationship was a necessary prerequisite for sexual intercourse. More than one-third of the girls said that fear of pregnancy was the main obstacle against having intercourse. From the attitude questions, we further conclude that the sexual field was discussed very rarely during conversations with the staff. Insecurity is also felt about the staff's attitudes to certain sexual behaviours, such as masturbation and petting. However, it is interesting that about 48 per cent judge their future possibilities for a sexual life with another person as being good. However, the investigation does not include questions about their own sexual experiences. Medical background variables such as the degree of mobility and need for technical aids have only been touched upon to a small extent as this aspect will be handled in an investigation in the near future. The pupils felt that sex education in the schools is desirable, but a clear majority wanted much more in this respect. Above all, they wished to know more about the ethics and psychology of sexual life and about technical aids to make coitus easier. Coitus positions and contraceptives had a high priority, as well as class discussions about the norms and values of sexual relationships. If the average school had a contraceptive-dispensing machine, nearly half of the pupils would use it.

The technical and practical obstacles to sexual relationships seemed to be the biggest problems preventing a sexual life, and it is upon this aspect that the working-group will concentrate some of their research in the future.

8

Sexual problems of the handicapped: the work of the Swedish Central Committee for Rehabilitation

INGER NORDQUIST

Since 1967 we have in Sweden discussed different ways to handle the issues and problems involved in the sexuality of the handicapped individual. A symposium took place in Stockholm in 1969. Social intercourse and the sexuality of people with locomotory difficulties were discussed because such handicaps can directly affect the sexual functions of some disabled men and women, such as those with paraplegia or tetraplegia, though perhaps not to the extent that many physicians and neurologists thought before they started research in this field. Only two pieces of research on this subject appear to have been undertaken in Sweden, in spite of the alleged broadmindedness of the Swede. But there are several English and American investigations, mostly about men with paraplegia, perhaps because coitus and the ability to achieve it are more demanding in man than in his partner.

No evidence was found to suggest that psychological problems in the sexual life of the handicapped were more prevalent than in the sexual life of the able-bodied. Instead, the problems involved were problems of communication and for some people those of a technical nature. The symposium also found that lack of knowledge and the belief that disabled people were also disabled in their ability to function sexually, to sire, to bear and to bring up children were largely evident amongst the disabled.

It is a view that exists from the beginning in some families with a handicapped child, and many parents seem to regard the child as sexless. And what serious difficulties of reduced self-esteem must this create in the child's future, when he or she seeks to establish an emotional relationship with someone of the opposite sex?

Such a situation also exists in boarding-schools for handicapped young people where proper information and advice about sexual matters is not available largely because of the ignorance of the school staff. In institutions there are seldom places where personal relationships can be pursued in private. In rehabilitation clinics there are no residential facilities for relatives, where, for instance, a visiting wife may go to bed with her spouse, who may well be a patient in such a clinic for quite a long time. The community at large sometimes reacts with hostility to an able-bodied person when he or she wishes to marry a handicapped person and for this we must in part blame the idealization of the body beautiful portrayed by advertisements, television and so on.

All these facts establish that the right and the opportunity of the handicapped individual to experience and to take part in a harmonious social and sexual life are considerably reduced.

For this reason the symposium came to the conclusion that knowledge about these problems must be disseminated and that it must be understood that the disabled are able to live a sexual life, that many people with locomotor difficulties can function sexually, that they want a sexual life, and that they need and why they need a normal sexual life. Indeed, so obvious are these facts that it is a pity that we have to explain about the human rights to love and to be loved. Evidently, the community considers it must take care of the physical needs of the disabled individual before his psychological needs can be solved. The majority to whom we spoke said that they had not thought about it before—that the handicapped also have sexual needs and impulses and want to fulfil them. This must represent a remarkable lack of imagination. As a result of the symposium a special book has been published for distribution to the various groups involved, such as the physically handicapped themselves, their families and staff involved with handicapped individuals. The book discusses sexual development from childhood to adulthood and the psychological and medical factors involved for the handicapped individual. The book examines the reactions of some parents to the birth of a handicapped child, how the child with a handicap realistically can be adjusted to the community, the freeing of the youth from parental ties, the environment of the home and institutions in relation to the sexual development of the handicapped child and teenager, sex education for pupils with handicaps, the general social adjustment of the adult person, the sexual life of man and woman with locomotor handicaps, contraception, marriage and divorce, and the problems of bringing up children when one or both parents are handicapped.

And a bibliography containing references to about 300 articles and books concerning relationships in general, inventories of sexual functions among people with different types of physical handicaps, psychological factors related to communications, and so on, has been made. National and international investigations are added to this bibliography as they arise.

Since January 1971 a special working-group of the SVCR has been studying sexuality of handicapped individuals of all types. The members of this working-group include Maj-Briht Bergstrom-Walan, Mrs Linnea Gardestrom, managing director of the State Council for the Handicapped, Bengt Lindqvist, a member of the research and development department of the Swedish Association of the Blind and Per Olov Lundberg, a neurologist working at the Academic Hospital in Uppsala.

The purposes of the working-group are:

(1) To collect information from all the various national

and international investigations undertaken in this field

(2) To disseminate this information to all those persons and organizations involved with the handicapped, schools, universities, physicians, psychologists, physiotherapists, occupational therapists, nurses, nurses assistants and indeed to anyone with an interest in this subject.

(3) To discuss the organization of special courses on this subject for professional workers and for the handicapped themselves.

(4) To consider the extent to which ordinary sex education really covers the needs of the handicapped person, ultimately to eliminate the need for special publications and books on sex for the handicapped.

(5) To correspond with international congresses in order to secure space in their programmes for discussion of all aspects of sexuality for the handicapped.

(6) To initiate and encourage other investigations in scientific research about the influence of different types of disability on sexual behaviour.

(7) To co-operate with members of different organizations for the handicapped and the Swedish Association for Sex Education. There have been discussions with professional staff from rehabilitation clinics and their handicapped patients together with teachers from boarding schools for handicapped young people and their students. And the working group will produce material for group discussions with handicapped individuals and their relatives.

The ultimate goal for this work is that an adult person, with or without a handicap, must be permitted to take responsibility for his or her own sexual life; must obtain information about how he or she can function sexually in spite of the handicap; must be given the opportunity to live the kind of sexual life he or she wishes, and finally should have a greater opportunity for communication and contact with other people and be able to choose his or her partner.

9

Young adults with cerebral palsy in Denmark: an investigation into some sexual problems

SVEN BRANT AND TORBEN V. HANSEN

A traditionally open-minded and secular—though not exactly immoral—attitude in the majority of the Danish population might eliminate some of the difficulties encountered in studies of human sexual behaviour; we all know how individual needs and feelings may cause conflicts in relation to both other individuals as well as to society, its traditional rules, its rulers and their political interests. Informative studies about sexual behaviour in young Danish people, both females (Kirsten Auken in 1953) and males (Preben Hertoft in 1968) have been undertaken during the last two decades. These publications do, however, refer to physically able persons.

It has been the general opinion that sex appeal very much depends upon a personality which perceives his (or her) own worth and rarely suffers from the risk of being discarded because of aberations from general standards of external or internal beauty or charm. For such reasons, as well as for others of a more technical nature, sexual needs might be expected to be less satisfied among those persons in whom a physical handicap may appear quite obvious, and although the persons concerned might 'hide an angel in his heart'. The preliminary study was limited to a small group of twenty-two persons and for this reason only very tentative conclusions can be made.

Material

Subjects for investigations were selected from the Cerebral Palsy Clinic at the Orthopedic Hospital in Copenhagen, seventeen years of age and over. Mild cases of cerebral palsy and youngsters of low intelligence were excluded. Also excluded were a few probands, who—according to our recorded data—had demonstrated obvious character and behaviour problems. Thus the primary material was selected according to what might well be criticized as a personal judgment, but it was felt that the studies must be limited to such persons in whom problems could be expected to be due primarily to handicap and not to other factors.

Forty persons were contacted by letter, inviting them to assist in a Danish study undertaken by interview. The interviewer was himself a young male athetoid, well able to establish suitable contact with other handicapped people. A short questionnaire supplemented the interview. Unfortunately, only fifteen out of the forty responded positively to the invitation. A further seven probands were therefore added through other sources, some of them because they were married to probands of our initial selection. This produced a total of twenty-two answers and interviews. This lack of willingness to participate might, of course, be explained in several ways, but is out of character with the otherwise high degree of responsibility shown by non-handicapped Danes approached for similar purposes. It may express the shyness and possible lack of sexual interest or experience among young persons with cerebral palsy. It may also indicate the severity of emotional, unclarified and eventually guilt-laden engagement in sexual affairs. One can only guess. Shyness was admitted by one girl, who offered a girlfriend, less shy, as a substitute! Fortunately, she was acceptable, because she too was cerebral palsied.

Results

For these reasons the facts are few in number and the conclusions that may be drawn correspondingly limited. The sexes were equally represented in our material of twenty-two persons with cerebral palsy. Persons with athetosis and para-tetraplegia were over-represented compared with hemiplegias. As mentioned, most mild cases were excluded, since it was felt that a high percentage of those would adapt comparatively well to a normal social life. Unfortunately, all six athetoids in the study were males, a fact that makes correlations with other types of cerebral palsy unrealistic. The majority of the probands were aged twenty or over.

Since the possibility for privacy even in a family situation is of great importance for undisturbed sexual life, the study was interested in information about the age at which an individual room was acquired. Unfortunately, many urban Danish families grow up in small apartments designed only for childless couples. Only three males and one female among the sixteen who answered this question had been lucky enough to possess their own individual room, when puberty arrived. Three had never had their own room, and at least eight had to wait for several years before this degree of privacy had been acquired. The age of first menstruation as well as the age for nocturnal emission, either spontaneous or due to masturbation, did not seem to deviate from findings in non-handicapped subjects. In spite of the paucity of the figures, it was found, however, that the age for first intercourse was late when compared with Danish non-handicapped youngsters. For the males, this age varied from fifteen to forty-four years of age, with an average of twenty-four and a half. For the girls this difference was perhaps less obvious, though clearly indicated by the small sample. On the other hand, only two (male, eighteen and female, twenty-seven) had no experience at all.

The first intercourse in our twenty probands had been with non-handicapped people for 50 per cent of the cases, equally in males and females. The few more lasting sexual contacts had been between two handicapped people, although the mildly handicapped had been excepted from this rule.

An analysis of the reports taken down by the interviewer provided some useful information, though few conclusions could be drawn from it. A few comments of the ten male probands are worth comment. With one exception—a boy of eighteen—all handicapped males expressed a strong need for sexual experience. This seems to be satisfied mostly through masturbation. One severely handicapped athetoid boy was not able even to achieve this, but was able, occasionally, to buy assistance from girls in his area. Six probands —all over twenty years of age—had intercourse only at an interval of several months with casual or sometimes 'professional' partners. Only three were married and had frequent intercourse. Two unmarried expressed their emotional reluctance against sexual contact with another handicapped partner, which was apparently only accepted as a solution to an emotional emergency. On the other hand, two couples—both handicapped to a mild or moderate degree—seemed to feel happy and satisfied with their situation.

It was felt—by studying some interviews—that the success of sporadic sexual experiences of a severely handicapped, cerebral palsied man might be more dependent upon his intellectual and emotional talents than upon his appearance, his charm and sex appeal than on his handicap. But it is evident that the restricted chance of establishing a more stable sexual relationship with a girlfriend was a considerable frustration to most of the severely handicapped men interviewed. Sublimation in hobbies, art or literature did not satisfy this need.

Unquestionably, some men have a greater need for sexual contact than others, and the impression was gained that cerebral palsied men are no exception to this rule. Such handicapped men experiencing a strong erotic tension could be spared much suffering if their needs could be gratified in a way acceptable to society without causing harm to the population at large. Almost all probands favoured brothels, where their sexual needs could be satisfied, and which were staffed with good-hearted, understanding, well-respected ladies; a kind of 'salvation army', intelligently accepting a male human being with normal strong emotional needs for contact and physical love. The fear that greater emotional involvement leading to even more suffering and longing might result, seemed not to concern the male probands, although one stated that his sexual needs definitely increased after his first experience, without any proportionate permanent satisfaction.

The attitude of parents towards the sexual adventures of their handicapped youngsters was usually one of acceptance. The attitude of the parents of the partner—particularly when able-bodied—was less tolerant. This was based, however, in one case, on the false assumption that cerebral palsy was hereditary. The amount of sexual information at school had been equally poor. Some parents, according to the young men, may have rationalized their hesitation by referring to the conviction that 'he will never get married'.

Conclusions

In Denmark, clinics for 'exclusive personal massage' are widely accepted and openly advertised. The handicapped are offered much help with public support and for housing and transport. However, one may have some doubt—in spite of the much debated Danish open-mindedness in sexual affairs—whether such 'massage' may be accepted as important enough for the total well-being of our handicapped to motivate public economic support in the future. Perhaps the physically handicapped might arrive at a more acceptable solution to this very intricate and very serious problem through their own organizations and clubs.

10

The activities of the Committee on the Sexual Problems of the Disabled in Holland

H. D'OLIVAT

The Committee on the Sexual Problems of the Disabled is one of the committees of the Nederlandse Centrale Vereniging ter bevordering van de Revalidatie (NCVR) and operates within the framework of the health protection activities of that body. Some years ago this specialized work was taken in hand by the NCVR because of the growing interest in sex and the position it occupies in advertizing, literature and the arts, and the frankness with which it is discussed in the normal world. Naturally the institutions concerned with rehabilitation were equally affected by this trend and here, too, sex became a serious topic of discussion amongst the patients themselves, sometimes with, but more usually without the knowledge of the staff of the institution. Eventually these matters attracted the attention of staff and management and examination showed that the problems and the extent of ignorance were greater and more serious than had been suspected.

Because of the prevalence of taboos, lack of education and the frustrations that exist in this field, few patients had the courage to ask questions and only in exceptional cases were the staff of rehabilitation centres asked to discuss these problems. The Committee's first conclusion was that rehabilitation could not really be regarded as complete unless sex problems were also taken fully into consideration.

The problems involved can best be divided into two main categories, psychological and instrumental. Disabled and able-bodied persons share the same psychological difficulties. Apart from those that arise from the lack of physical ability there are those difficulties that stem from the four prevailing conceptions of sexuality and sexual behaviour. These conceptions result from religious and moral influences and may be defined as follows:

a. As food serves to ensure the survival of the individual, sex serves to ensure the survival of the human race. The sole purpose of sex is to ensure the perpetuation of mankind. Reproduction is the only fundamental purpose of sex.

b. But sex is also love-play and the satisfaction of feelings between two partners. The usual relationship is that of marriage, within which sex is permitted. But a relationship between unmarried persons, and homosexual relationships, may lead to this love-play and subsequent satisfaction. The relationship is, however, an essential condition. The longer and better two persons know each other, the more intimate is their relationship.

c. Sex is a human need that must be satisfied in the same way that hunger must be appeased. For this, one person needs another whether there is a relationship or not. One uses the other in order to satisfy himself. Prostitution is an example of this. There is no question of a continued relationship except for the purpose of sexual satisfaction.

d. Sex is a need that must be satisfied. When a relationship with another person is not possible, the individual satisfies himself. Masturbation has been responsible for many feelings of guilt amongst young persons. It used to be the subject of dire threats of fearful diseases and divine retribution, with the result that many are still obsessed by feelings of guilt arising from youthful peccadilloes.

It is the psychological aspects of the relationship, with another person or with oneself, that are important. For the blind and the deaf, who are not genitally disabled, the problem of sexual relationship is of great importance. For example, a blind boy who could draw by touch drew his mother with her breasts on her back. The discovery that he had drawn the picture wrongly obviously inhibited his capacity for relationships with girls. A blind person's perception largely consists of tactile sensibility and tactile contact is precisely that aspect of sexual activity which normally does not take place until the relationship has been established, and certainly not when the couple first meet, as a way of getting to know each other. The blind cannot see the photographs, prints, paintings, newspapers and magazines available to sighted persons, in which nudity is often depicted and to which a further dimension can be added by means of one's own imagination.

What does a man look like? What does a woman look like? The literary screen through which all braille matter passes, and which is operated by sighted persons and by instructors for the blind, tends to ensure that only 'respectable' and 'polished' literature appears in braille. This is a particular kind of censorship.

The deaf too have their own particular kind of impediment to relationship. Love-play involves sounds and words, which complement the action, alter behaviour or attitude or give rise to a pause, all because, with the aid of his sense of hearing, one person is aware of what is happening to the other. A deaf person who is constantly anxious lest he should react wrongly is bound to suffer the same anxiety in this situation because he cannot hear or adjust his behaviour to his hearing. The psychological aspects are not only very much concerned in the establishment of relationship: they are also involved in the diffidence and embarrassment, the taboos and norms, that inhibit free discussion about sex, with the result that physical ability may also be frequently affected. The instrumental aspects, which are closely related to the psychological ones, are of course of importance in physically disabled persons whose nervous system has been damaged and where the functions of the brain and lower part of the body are disturbed. To the large group of people suffering from paralysis of the lower body, possibly as a result of an accident, with consequent loss of the use of the legs and genital organs, the physical problems are severe.

It is precisely this loss that focuses attention on sex and sexual activity. The first thing most people want to know after an accident—apart from the question of survival—is whether they will still be capable of sexual activity. The Committee on the Sexual Problems of the Disabled, which owed its existence to the growing awareness of the problems existing in this field, was now faced with the task of sorting a mass of reports and views that had been submitted but which above all lacked factual background. Solutions, both long and short term, had to be found and a programme of work had to be set up.

Objectives

Principal objectives would have to be formulated to take stock of all the facts relating to sex and sexual activity among the disabled, and to study ways in which help could be given by means of information, discussions and exchange of views, both to the disabled themselves and to those around them.

Literature

Little literature had been published on this subject and information was sought both at home and abroad. Information from the Spastics Society in London was interesting but there the complex of sexual problems is regarded as forming part of the 'marriage problems', whilst in the Netherlands the tendency is rather to speak of 'relationship problems', i.e. not restricted exclusively to marriage problems, but extending also to relationships such as exist between unmarried couples and persons of the same sex. Although the literature did not contribute much towards the solution of the problems, the Committee felt that the contacts that were established in this way were of great value, since they showed clearly that solutions to the same problems were being sought and the same aspects of the subject being discussed in other countries, too. A start has been made on documentation which would ultimately provide a source of information for doctors, nurses, guardians, parents, partners, family members and the disabled themselves. It is intended to publish notices concerning this documentation at some time in the future in the *Tijdschrift voor Revalidatie*.

Scientific study

There is also an obvious need for a scientific socio-psychological study of the question. After consultations within the Committee, it was decided to entrust this scientific study to the Instituut voor Toegepast Sociaalpsychologisch en Agologisch Onderzoek of the University of Amsterdam (INTAGON). The study will extend over some two years and a report will be published on its conclusion. The possibility is being discussed of publishing the report, together with comments and a few additional articles, in a scientific paperback series. The study will consist of a number of interviews with disabled people conducted in discussion groups by the staff of the Instituut voor Voorlichtingskunde en Communicatie in Rotterdam. These discussions will be based on a questionnaire using the interview techniques devised by sociologists with experience in this particular area of work.

Direct help

It may happen that a rehabilitation centre suddenly feels the need to form a discussion group to discuss sex, or that a group is formed spontaneously for this purpose by patients. In this case, there would at the same time be a need for a group leader to conduct the group's sessions.

It was discovered that one or two institutions had group leaders who had been trained to work with groups of able-bodied people set up to obtain information about disabled persons so that, if necessary, they could also offer their services in this sphere. It was appreciated that a discussion group with disabled people was a rather different matter from giving information to non-disabled.

It soon became clear that speech defects demanded time and patience whilst the visual confrontation with the severely disabled could well inhibit the necessary contact with inexperienced group leaders. The special training and discussion programme included the following topics: technical aids (general) for the disabled; the medical, social and psychological aspects of disablement; the environment of the disabled in the rehabilitation centre or other institutions, and in the outside world; practice in conducting discussions with disabled people. These training courses were provided in various rehabilitation centres, at a protected workplace and in a training centre for the disabled. The study, the inquiries and the documentation clearly had to be set in motion as soon as possible. In June 1970 this training was concluded and contact was made with the various institutions for the disabled emphasizing the need for setting up discussion groups. Once this need had been established, group leaders were set to work, distributed through the country in such a way that practically all provinces and regions were able to make use of them. The fees and expenses of group leaders are paid from a budget to which the rehabilitation centres themselves contribute.

Direct and personal assistance

Extensive publicity cannot yet be given, since facilities for direct individual help and information are not yet available. Nevertheless, letters are received from private persons as a result of what little has been published, and one member of the Committee, a doctor, has taken on the task of dealing with these personal inquiries from disabled people and acting as a referral agent.

The consideration of direct personal assistance led to the formation of local and regional teams of advisers to provide 'individual' disabled persons, normally those living at home, with the help and information they need. A local or regional team could be of great value not only to the disabled themselves, but also to their partners, parents, guardians, and acquaintances, who need confidential and expert advice on matters concerning sex, sexual activity and heredity. The composition of these teams would reflect the nature and requirements of the local and regional situations and would consist of members of the staffs of institutions concerned with rehabilitation. Such a team would include a doctor specializing in rehabilitation, a family doctor, a clergyman and a social worker—for sociological and religious factors in the local or regional situation play a part. The teams must be able to call upon the Committee on the Sexual Problems of the Disabled for documentation and assistance from such specialists, as geneticians, psychologists, andrologists and psychiatrists.

Publicity

Members of the Committee have on a number of occasions given talks on radio and television, for much store is placed on good publicity. The case files would with a little editing produce much material suitable for publication, but great care must obviously be taken, particularly as this might create a demand for help that could not immediately be met due to the present shortage of staff. The Committee hopes through its work to promote that very human happiness which comes from a healthy sex life.

11

Therapeutic possibilities for physically handicapped males with sexual disorders

TON M. C. M. SCHELLEN

Marriage of the physically handicapped male to a female in good bodily health imposes a severe strain on the latter, a strain which, as time goes on, often appears to be greater than her psychical endurance and in which possibly the failure to become pregnant weighs heavier in the long run than the lack of normal marital relationship. In spite of the fact that on this particular subject our experience is limited, one notices that frequently a physically sound partner passes lightly over the sexual handicap of the other. What is more certain is the situation that arises when a female marries a sterile male whose sexual functions are otherwise normal. Sooner or later the female becomes keenly aware of a great desire for a child, a desire that often results in overstrain due to lack of sufficient diversion, matrimonial troubles ending in either divorce or extra-marital relationships, desexualization of the female, because 'it's no use at all', and desperate attempts to enforce pregnancy outside the marriage bed.

We all realize that everybody has a right to sexual relationship, but equally should the sexually handicapped male fully realize that he may unwillingly hurt his partner, an injustice which, if not properly discussed, will often have disastrous effects.

Maybe one of these days we shall know whether in general a marriage of a healthy female to a sexually handicapped male can be regarded as a sound and acceptable proposition. But it is far from certain what will be the solution to the problem of a marriage of two handicapped partners, particularly with regard to procreation, if this is possible. For the solution to these problems, the opinion and advice of a geneticist must be sought.

The procreative function

In general the handicapped male will know in advance that difficulty will be experienced in securing a conjugal relationship, whereas matters stand quite differently with regard to procreation, as many still maintain a dormant hope that they will be able to become fathers. Therefore comment must be made about the procreative functions. Due regard should be paid to spermatogenetic disorders caused by:

a. atrophy of the tubuli seminifori due to disturbance of the autonomic nervous system;
b. inhibition of spermatogenesis due to disordered thermo-regulation; disorders of the sperm transport system caused by ascending infection, in particular the adnexitis masculinim, resulting in an obstructive-azoospermia; the development of sperm-agglutinin, caused by a one-sided or two-sided obstruction, resulting in complete sterility.

Thus in many handicapped males, as indicated above, besides a disordered potentia coeundi there will also be a disordered potentia generandi, for which there is little or no possibility available for direct therapeutic aid. Operative therapy in cases of obstruction will mostly be contra-indicated because of recurrence of the obstruction caused by the infection, while the inducement of a spermatocele according to Schoysman is no longer applied. For this operative interference, performed in particular in cases of aplasia of the deferential system, a piece of the long saphenous vein may be used and placed on the caput of the epididymis, in order to create in this way a 'sperm room', from which sperm can be obtained to perform an AIH. Recently Schoysman himself announced at an 'andrologische Tagung' in Hamburg that because of lack of success he has ceased to apply this method. Since in all those cases in which there is still some spermatogenesis no hormonal influence whatsoever may be expected to be effective, the only alternatives left are adoption or donor insemination.

As to the Netherlands, in practice adoption is a difficult matter, due to the great demand and the small number of available children, independently of the question whether a family with a handicapped father will be the ideal place for a developing adopted child. This applies more or less to the so-called AID, about which the opinion in our country has become broader and more lenient than it was ten years ago.

Regarding the sexual functions

The impotentia erigendi: if, due to a traumatic lesion, the erection is insufficient or absent, while often the ejaculation is retained, substances with androgenic action can have a stimulating effect only when as a result of trophic disorders of the testes the cells of Leydig fail to function, causing an androgen deficiency. This is only rarely the case and these substances are administered too often, frequently with injurious effects. The preparation to be regarded as eminent in cases of disordered Leydig function is proviron, as it neither inhibits the hypophysis nor does it damage the liver. As to the administration of gonadotrophic hormones, there is seldom or never an indication for it.

Although in our clinic we have no experience with it, Dengrove's statement (February 1971) about the use of an artificial penis in case of erection disorders and premature ejaculation should not be ignored. The advantage of this artificial penis, compared with the non-erect penis enlarged by a thick condom, is that during the frictional motions an erection can still occur, because the friction can be transmitted via the artificial penis to the penis. Further advantages are that in this way during coitus the female can still be gratified and the male will forget his sexual insufficiency and will undertake coitus with more conviction and enthusiasm.

In conclusion it must be stated that as to the administration of prostigmine, the intrethecal application is more successful than the oral. The objection to intrathecal administration is that it may be dangerous and the therapeutic effect is only of brief duration.

Impotentia ejaculandi: frequently, when the potentia erigendi is maintained, there is no ejaculation and hence no orgasm, while it is also known that ejaculation may occur retrogradely, the so-called 'plaisir sec', making the ejaculate flow into the bladder. In these cases one can try to use the ejaculate from the bladder for artificial insemination, taking care beforehand that the pH in the bladder is favourable, for if this is too low the sperm cells will be dead. Unfortunately those so handicapped often suffer from a recurrent infection of the urinary tract, so that the ejaculate, voided in the bladder, is unfit for artificial insemination. There are data in the literature on electro-stimulation to induce ejaculation. Whereas in veterinary medicine much experience has been obtained with this method, this is still hardly the case in human medicine. According to the method applied by Rowan, electrodes are placed in the rectum and on the sacral vertebrae. The results obtained are not yet sufficiently encouraging for frequent clinical application.

A simpler method, with which we ourselves have four years' experience, is electromechanical vibrator therapy. Initially we applied this method only to patients with non-organic ejaculation disorders, when some erection was maintained and when there were nocturnal emissions. The results were amazing. In about 90 per cent of the cases ejaculation could be induced, in about 45 per cent pregnancy via insemination, while about 35 per cent of the patients were able to proceed to ejaculation via a normal coitus. A short time ago we started applying this method also to patients with organic ejaculation disorders. The results, though less spectacular than in the first-mentioned group, are still encouraging. The method is simple, harmless and not repulsive.

Summary and conclusions

The improved facilities of rehabilitation have confronted the medical practitioner also with the problem of the sexually handicapped. For the time being there are only a few therapeutic possibilities, though some described methods may be encouraging. More important than these aids is the guidance of the sexually handicapped on their way to manhood, when making their decision to marry or not to marry and whether or not to aspire to parenthood.

12

Genetic counselling

C. O. CARTER

We are concerned with the general principles of genetic counselling, and their application to cerebral palsy. The objectives of genetic counselling are three: to give accurate replies to enquiries from patients or parents of a patient about a risk of recurrence of the disease in children or further children; to alert the medical profession to special risks of a disease before a child is born so that early diagnosis may be made and treatment started early; in the long term to reduce the birth frequency of disorders which are wholly or in large part genetically determined.

In the case of cerebral palsy it is the first objective that is the important one at present. The general principle in the United Kingdom in genetic counselling on risks to children is that parents or patients are entitled to accurate information on the risks involved, but that any decision whether to take the risk or not rests with the enquirer. Where it is the normal parents who are asking for information, this is straightforward. Clearly the principle may need some modification when the patient himself is the enquirer and the patient's handicap is such that he cannot on his own make a responsible decision about having children. Where this is the case, however, there will be social reasons additional to any genetic ones why the pateint should not have children.

The two essential requirements for making an accurate

estimate of a recurrence risk are a good family history and an accurate diagnosis. The latter is perhaps the more important and, where an accurate diagnosis of a specific condition may be made, the mode of inheritance has usually already been established and precise risks may be stated. For example, Sjogren's syndrome of spastic paraplegia, ichtyosis and erythrodermia has been shown to be an autosomal recessive disorder and the parents may be told the recurrence risk is 1 in 4, that is 3 to 1 for a normal child in any subsequent pregnancy. However, apparently similar clinical entities may be inherited in more than one way and sometimes a family tree by itself may indicate clearly the mode of inheritance in a particular family. Thus in the family described by Wolplast in 1943 with five males affected with congenital non-progressive spastic paraplegia and mental retardation, inheritance is clearly X-linked; a family with congenital spastic paraplegia and mental retardation reported by Book is clearly autosomal recessive.

The risks that may be stated to the enquirer fall into three classes: the first is when one can say that the risk is no more than the random risk for any pregnancy; second, those where there is a high risk—say 1 in 2 or 1 in 4 or at least 1 in 10; third, those in which there is a moderate risk, in the sense that it is less than 1 in 10, but still many times more than the random risk in the general population.

The first class of risk—no more than the random risk—applies obviously when the child's handicap is due to an environmental agent that is not likely to be repeated, for example rubella embryopathy or toxoplasmosis. Much the same risk applies, and this is less well known, when the child's handicap is genetically determined, but the genetic anomaly is due to fresh mutation and there is no genetic abnormality in either parent. Most chromosome anomalies are seen as fresh mutations and this is nearly always the case when the anomaly is an aneuploidy, that is when there is present an extra chromosome or a chromosome is missing. This is true for example of some 98 per cent of cases of Down's syndrome. There is no substantial increased risk to later brothers and sisters of the patient except where the child has an unbalanced structural chromosome anomaly which is also present, but in the balanced state, in one or other parent. Most instances of patients with severe dominant conditions are also due to fresh mutations. Almost all cases of Apert's syndrome, that is acrocephalosyndactyly, are due to fresh mutations, and a majority of cases even of tuberose sclerosis are due to fresh dominant mutations. In tuberose sclerosis, however, if one or other parent has any cutaneous stigmata of the disease, the chance of recurrence in later children is 1 in 2.

High risk situations, 1 in 10 or greater, apply when a structural chromosome anomaly which has been inherited from one or other parent is involved, or when a mutant gene of large effect is involved and one or both parents carry the gene. The commonest chromosomal situation in practice carrying a high risk is where a child has Down's syndrome with 46 chromosomes including a D/G translocation, and the clinically normal mother has 45 chromosomes and a D/G translocation. The recurrence risk of Down's syndrome here is of the order of 1 in 6. In general wherever there is a structural abnormality, as for example in the 'cri-du-chat' syndrome with a deletion of the short arm of chromosome 5, chromosomal studies are necessary to see if there is a similar but balanced chromosome anomaly in one or other parent. The actual risk of a liveborn handicapped child in these situations can only be established by empirical observation. But in the case of a woman with a balanced translocation involving the short arm of chromosome 5 and another chromosome, two of three possibly viable genotypes in the children will have severe handicap. With conditions due to mutant genes of large effect these will usually but not invariably be progressive conditions, and the risk given can be based on simple Mendelian theory once the mode of inheritance has been established by an adequate family study. In the case of fully dominant conditions, for example some of the later onset forms of progressive spastic ataxia or Huntington's chorea, the general rule is that there is little or no risk to the later brothers and sisters of the patient but there is a 1 in 2 risk to the offspring of the first affected individual and to offspring of all later patients in the family. Difficulty only arises where there is a late onset as in Huntington's chorea, so that it is uncertain in early adult life whether an individual member of a family has inherited the gene or not and also in conditions with very variable manifestation such as dystrophia myotonia. The discovery of special tests in such conditions to distinguish early those who have or have not inherited the condition will be of great help in genetic counselling. With recessive conditions such as classical Friedreich's ataxia, or metachromatic leucodystrophy, the situation is quite different from that with dominants. There is a 1 in 4 risk to later brothers and sisters of a patient even when he or she is the first person to be affected in the family, but little risk to the offspring of patients or any other relatives of the patient. Even with a locally common condition, for example phenylketonuria in Ireland (where it has a birth frequency of about 5,000), the risk to the offspring of treated survivors of having the genetic condition is only of the order of 1 in 35. In this case there is also the environmental risk of brain damage to the child from the mother's raised phenylaline level unless this is well controlled. With X-linked conditions such as Pelizaeus-Merzbacher disease, in general the important risk is the 1 in 2 chance of disease to the sons of heterozygous carrier women and the 1 in 2 risk to the daughters of such women of being a carrier. The difficulty here is usually in knowing whether or not a particular woman in a family is a carrier. A woman who has had an affected son and has any other affected male relative is certainly a carrier, as is a woman who is the daughter of an affected male. But a woman who has only one affected brother has about a 1 in 3 chance of being a carrier. The other 1 in 3 chance is that her son has been affected by a fresh mutation and then there is little risk to any further children of that woman. Obviously special tests to distinguish carrier women are most valuable here and fortunately it seems likely that usually it will be much easier as well as practically more important to pick up women who are carriers of X-linked mutant genes than those who carry autosomal recessive genes. This is because the inactivation of one X-chromosome in women means that in many cells a carrier woman will have the X-chromosome with a mutant gene as the only active X-chromosome. The function of these cells will be affected. An example of such useful though incomplete detection of carriers of X-linked mutant genes is the use of plasma creatine kinase levels in relation to the severe X-linked form of muscular dystrophy.

Moderate risks of recurrence apply with a number of common conditions whose aetiology is not yet fully known. In some instances the reason for the moderate risk is that the genetic element in the aetiology of the condition is polygenic. That is to say that those affected are at one extreme of the normal distribution of genetic predisposition for the condition and an additional environmental trigger has tipped the balance towards malformation or disease. This is the aetiology of many common malformations such as cleft lip and palate, and probably also of the neural tube malformations, myelocoele, encephalocoele and anencephaly. In other instances the reason for the moderate risk is that the patients are heterogeneous and include many with purely environmental determination and little risk of recurrence, but also a few with single gene determination and a high risk of recurrence, but which cannot be recognized clinically. To establish the risk here what is needed is a well-planned and large scale family study to give an empirical risk figure. It must be realized that in these situations the risk will vary from one family to another, but since no differentiation can be made in advance between these groups, the empirical risk figure is the best one to give and is useful in practice.

In the case of cerebral palsy the empirical risk of recurrence appears to be of the order of 1 or 2 per cent with an additional risk of say 2 per cent of mental retardation without true cerebral palsy. There is clearly a need for further family studies and these will become increasingly precise as more of the specific aetiologies of this group of conditions are determined.

Summarizing now more specifically the main points about genetic counselling for cerebral palsy; if there is a clear-cut environmental cause, for example, a hemiplegia following on measles or pertussis encephalomyelitis, or an otitis media, there is only the random risk of cerebral palsy in either a later brother or sister of the index patient or in the children of a patient. There must, however, be a clear-cut indication of any environmental cause. Most histories of 'birth injury' are inconclusive. If there are indications that a mutant gene of large effect is involved—and the indication may come either from a precise diagnosis, as in the Sjogren-Larsson syndrome or the Louis-Bar syndrome of ataxia-telangiectasia (also recessive), the recessive Marinesco-Sjogren syndrome of congenital spino-cerebellar-ataxia with cataract and mental retardation, or from a typical pedigree—then the risks of recurrence are those of a dominant, recessive or X-linked condition. These risks may be high: 1 in 2 or 1 in 4 for either a later brother or sister or for a child, depending on the exact mode of inheritance involved. These cases will be rare. Undoubtedly, however, there are instances of single gene determined cases which we cannot at present distinguish. In the case of either spastic diplegia or choreoathetosis where the parents are first cousins, in a population where as in most parts of Europe the general rate of first cousin marriage is low, the risk to later brothers and sisters of patients must approach the 1 in 4 given by recessive inheritance. In addition, where there is dyskinetic cerebral palsy due to kernicterus from rhesus incompatibility, the recurrence risk for later sibs will of course be high.

Where there are no indications of a specific environmental aetiology and no indications of determination by a mutant gene of large effect, an empirical risk figure may be given. This figure may be taken as a small one, of the order of 2 to 3 per cent for most forms of non-specific cerebral palsy and less than this for hemiplegia. Further empirical studies are needed, but the findings for example of Ingram in Edinburgh may be taken as representative. With seventy-five index patients with hemiplegia he found that two sibs out of 144 brothers and sisters had cerebral palsy; both had spastic diplegia. With seventy-five index patients with congenital diplegia he found that of ninety-six brothers and sisters three had cerebral palsy; of these two had diplegia (these were twins) and one congenital hemiplegia. With twelve patients with ataxia diplegia, one was a member of a dominant family with non-progressive ataxia diplegia, but the other eleven had twenty-four unaffected brothers and sisters. With seventeen patients with dyskinesis none of twenty-four brothers and sisters was affected.

SUNY GENESEO
HV1559.E8 P47
YGMM
Personal relationships, the handicapped
3 0260 00142401 3